...strom & Mary O. Sundstrom

...es

Everything About Heritage and Puppy Care, as well as
Understanding Competitive Events and Dog Shows

Filled with Full-color Photographs
Illustrations by Michele Earle-Bridges

D0191634

BARRON'S

CONTENTS

THE COLLIE: AN HONORED HERITAGE

Of all purebred dogs, the Collie is one of the breeds most often written about. Few other breeds have so captured the public's affection.

Little wonder that the Collie's legendary reputation has provided inspiration to writers and artists, the movies, television, and literature. Hardly a generation passes that does not fall in love with the Collie. The beauty and character qualities of the Collie have been recognized by people of all ages. The Collie's integrity and courage are an inseparable part of its honored heritage.

A delightful sense of humor, intelligence, intense loyalty, and love for mankind has made the Collie a welcome family member. The Collie's readiness to defend its family has been demonstrated by countless, well-attested incidents. Collie heroics are accepted as almost standard performance, and the Collie has been named repeatedly in the national dog hero

Generations of careful breeding have turned the Collie into the beautiful specimen it is today.

awards each year. The modern Collie is faithful to this tradition.

Origin

The Collie's origin in the border area of Scotland and northern England was evolutionary. Though its early history is vague, breed historians suppose that dogs introduced by the Roman invaders about 500 B.C. eventually bred with local herding dogs. Later, the agricultural revolution of the mid-eighteenth century gave rise to the selective breeding of domestic animals. When farm animals were confined to walled or fenced pastures, this move from open fields to enclosures had a marked effect on both livestock and the breeding of farmers' dogs. Among other shepherd-type dogs, two varieties of Collies evolved—the rough- and the smooth-coated Collie. The Collies were used for herding and as guardians and later as companions and show dogs. With broad, short heads

TIP

Names

Consider carefully the name you give your Collie if it is to be registered with the American Kennel Club. This name may be different than his "call name." The longer and more unusual name is more likely to be approved than, for example, a plain "Blaze" or "Rex."

and heavy ears, the early Collies were smaller than the modern one that began to emerge around 1886.

Rough and Smooth Varieties

In addition to the well-known "Lassie"-type of Collie, there is a smooth variety. In Smooth Collies the coat is short and dense, and requires much less grooming. Sometimes, Smooth Collies may appear smaller because of the difference in coat, but they are actually identical to their Rough brothers and sisters and have the same kindly temperament and intelligence.

It is an open question whether the Smooth Collie was a parallel development of the Rough Collie or was developed as a separate breed. The Rough specialized in sheep, while the Smooth was used extensively with cattle. Generations of careful breeding have turned the Collie into the beautiful specimen it is today, with the Rough's elegant coat and the Smooth's distinctive outline, increased size, and tulip ears. Both the Smooth and the Rough have the same structure,

characteristics, and temperaments. Breed historians declare that during the mid-1800s northern England's Smooth Collies resembled the present type more closely than the Rough Collie. Once used as a herder and drover of sheep and cattle to market, the smooth-coated Collie of today is a descendant of one of the oldest types of pastoral dogs.

"Colley Dog"

Many of the early Collies were black and white in color. It was believed that less white color denoted the purity of the breed. The darkness of the breed's coat may have derived from the Anglo-Saxon word for black—"col." The Collie's name was originally spelled "colley." Scotland's black-faced sheep were once called "colleys," and the dog that herded them and drove them came to be known as "colley dog." William Shakespeare used the word in its meaning of black in reference to the "Collied night" in *A Midsummer Night's Dream*. "Coll, our dog" was mentioned by Geoffrey Chaucer, who is the source for the word *coal*. Other writers have suggested that the white band around the Collie's neck is a natural collar. Another historian has said that the word *Collie* is derived from the Gaelic tongue, since the word for a whelp or puppy is *cuilean* in that ancient language.

The Popular Collie

From the Scottish lowlands where it originated and has a long history as a herding dog, the Collie emerged as a distinct and popular purebred dog in the middle of the nineteenth century. England's Queen Victoria became enamored of the Collie and claimed the breed

Originating in the border area of Scotland and northern England, Collies have a long history as herding dogs.

The Collie gained its contemporary popularity through books, movies, and television.

as a companion dog at Scotland's Balmoral Castle. Returning to London with the royal family, the breed gained wide popular acceptance and began its ascendancy as a favored dog in both the United Kingdom and abroad.

Collies in America

Collies used for herding and guarding were brought to America and Canada by migrating settlers for use on farms and ranches.

Collies gained great public favor as companion dogs in the United States and were tremendously successful on the show dog circuit. Benefiting one of the oldest breeds, the Collie Club of America was organized in 1886 as the national parent club and became a member of the American Kennel Club in 1888.

Inevitably, Collies imported from Great Britain were the basis of American breeding stock and provided the majority of show dog entries in subsequent decades. The most

Rough-coated blue merle Collie.

famous Collie fancier at the turn of the century was financier and industrialist J. Pierpont Morgan. His Cragston Kennels cut a wide swath in the awards at the biggest American shows in the 1890s. By the end of World War I, domestic Collie breeders were primary in the show ring.

Book, Movie, and TV Fame

The Collie's reputation in America became fixed in public popularity with its immortalization on the pages of Albert Payson Terhune's novels, articles, and short stories about his Sunnybank Collies early in the twentieth century. Terhune's glowing prose in books titled *Bruce*, *Grey Dawn*, and *Lad: A Dog* fixed in the public's eye the vision of the Collie as a dog of unquestioned courage and intelligence, as well as an uncanny understanding of humans.

The contemporary Collie's popularity soared worldwide with the beloved 1945 technicolor adventure film classic, *Lassie Come Home*.

Collies love people, watching over their family as a good shepherd.

British author Eric Knight's novel was the Collie star's first movie and was followed by a succession of Lassie films. Both Terhune and Knight described the Collie "as loyal a dog as you will ever know." From their pages and through movies and, later, television, the Collie has become an American folk hero.

Perhaps the Collie's greatest popularity occurred with the globally serialized television programs featuring a succession of Lassies. Trained by the late Rudd Weatherwax, the Lassie tradition continues with his son, Rob, who is preparing the ninth-generation Lassie for film and television stardom. The clever Collie has actually been around more than a half century. In 2002, Lassie was voted the most popular animal ever in a film.

The Collie Companion

Collie owners vouch for the breed's keen sense of understanding. They are gregarious and inquisitive by nature, and masters at playfulness and pranks. Like many of the herding breeds, Collies have exceptional intelligence and sterling character. They excel as faithful, gentle, sweet-natured dogs with a great depth of affection. They love people and have a renowned willingness to bestow affection with an inherent desire to please. Admirers of Collies are drawn to their tolerant nature.

Collies are by no means timid dogs. Sensing imminent danger, they are instantly alert. It is not unusual—and a shared disposition with other

A Collie is a loyal companion.

breeds—to hear reports confirming Collies' unerring awareness of thunderstorms hours before the sky hints of approaching heavy weather. Unusual restless and nervous actions accompanied by fast breathing are Collies' unfailing telltale signs of looming storms and of earthquakes. We had such a Collie at one time; ironically, her name was Halamar's Stormy Dawn.

Although Collies are a medium breed—females are 22 to 24 inches (56–61 cm) at the shoulder and males 24 to 26 inches (61–66 cm)—they do not require a large amount of space to feel at home—but they do need an occasional romp or at least a daily walk. Coupled with the exercise that is a boon to both of you, teaching your Collie to walk or run on leash is of benefit to all.

There is an indisputable reward for the Collie owner: a Collie is a friend that makes a human feel totally acceptable. Nothing can make you feel prouder than a neighbor or stranger stopping to greet your Collie, exclaiming how lovely it is and how lucky you are. The only thing better than owning a Collie is owning two.

Watching the interaction of an inquisitive Collie and its owner is a fascinating experience.

A Collie Tale

Halamar's the Patriot was a large sable and white Collie that decided early in life he was to be our gatekeeper. He rarely barked or made any type of sound. We believed he knew his very size made it unnecessary. Anyone could come into the yard and get almost to the door before Pat would make his presence known. He merely appeared to the guest and took his or her arm gently in his mouth, making it very clear he wished the person to remain still until one of us said it was all right to enter. The routine would repeat itself when the person left our house, unless we walked our guest through the door and to his or her car. He never growled or was aggressive; indeed, he wagged his tail, pleased that he had accomplished a great task.

COLLIE PUPPIES

An outgoing puppy, one that comes to you out of curiosity, one that seems confident with littermates as well as alone, should indicate a secure and happy pup. A young pup with bright eyes, healthy-looking coat, and a good weight will tell you that it is off to a fine start.

How to Find Your Puppy

Locating a Collie puppy can sometimes be a frustrating experience depending on your location and, in some cases, the time of year you begin your search. There are several good alternatives to consider:

✔ Ask a local veterinarian for breeder references. Presumably, he or she will have knowledge of such breeders, having seen and treated their dogs.

✔ Check an area all-breed kennel club, sometimes listed in the telephone book yellow pages. Their representative can put you in touch with member Collie breeders or tell you about an area Collie Club.

✔ The American Kennel Club in New York (see Information, page 92). They will put you in touch with the Collie Club of America. They can give you information on breeders in your state.

Talking to knowledgeable people, attending local dog shows and obedience trials, and asking questions about Collies in general will be of help to you in finding and selecting the right puppy.

Today the Internet offers a useful tool—but remember that the information offered may or may not be factual.

Sometimes you must be prepared to wait for a puppy. For instance, you may be referred to an excellent breeder in your area who does not have a litter of puppies at the time you call, and does not have a litter planned in the near future, but he or she will usually be happy to give you the name of someone with puppies for sale.

Collie puppies that breeders feel are the most likely candidates for showing are kept by the breeder for further perpetuation of the family traits, or sold to a show home. If you are interested in obtaining a show prospect puppy, your breeder can become your best and most valuable resource. The price for a show dog is significantly more than you will pay for a companion dog and the seller will want some assurances that you will indeed exhibit the Collie sold to you.

An alert, confident, and happy puppy is an ideal choice.

Collie puppies are naturally curious and even tempered.

Older Puppies

Some breeders have older puppies and dogs they want to place in good homes. Young puppies require a great deal of concentrated care, so an older one may be a good choice in homes where there are very young children or where both adults are away for most of the day.

Collie Rescue

Another excellent place to consider acquiring a Collie is a Collie rescue group. These dogs have been offered foster homes while permanent homes are being sought. Collie breeders and friends of the breed take Collies into their homes for a variety of reasons. Many Collies in this program are older dogs but there are numerous happy stories of how successful this alliance has proved to be. To find out about Collie rescue programs, contact community

animal shelters, local breeders, and veterinarians. There are Collie rescue programs all across the United States.

Purchasing any dog should be viewed as a long-term commitment. A loyal and loving companion over a lifespan of many years should be your goal. An informed and knowledgeable buyer is an important factor in achieving this objective.

Before contact is made with a breeder that has puppies for sale, there are a number of questions you should answer:

✔ Will this be a Collie for the entire family?
✔ Is this the breed everyone has agreed upon?
✔ Have you factored into the family budget the cost of veterinarian care, food, toys, leash, collar, grooming tools, training classes, boarding fees, or home care when the family takes a vacation without the dog?

✔ Who will be the primary caregiver, responsible for feeding, exercise, and cleaning up?

Decisions for the Buyer to Make

Male or Female?

Sometimes there is a strong preference for a puppy of one gender or the other. Both sexes make excellent companions and having a closed mind on the subject can limit your choices, causing you to pass over an excellent pup for that reason alone. Unless you intend to enter the world of show dogs and are entertaining thoughts of becoming a breeder—both areas better left to knowledgeable persons in the field—keeping your options open for both sex and color will bring your search for a puppy to a faster conclusion. Selecting a puppy on the merits of personality and temperament should please you more in the long run.

Both male and female Collies alike grow up to be gentle and loving companions with an innate desire to please. Males are usually larger in size than their sisters but by only a few inches. Both sexes will shed their coats at least once a year and both will need a weekly grooming to keep them looking their best.

Spaying and neutering: Whichever sex you choose, spaying or neutering at an appropriate age should be a serious consideration. This procedure does not affect the personality or the behavior in any significant manner. Talking with a veterinarian about this option before purchasing a dog of any age is a good idea.

Although similar in appearance, all puppies have different personalities.

Many breeders today will ask that new owners alter their puppies to prevent unwanted litters and indiscriminate breeding, contributing to the problem of overpopulation.

Females not spayed will come into season approximately every six months. A season or heat lasts generally about three weeks. Close supervision must be given during this time as the scent of a female in heat attracts male dogs from near and far with only one objective in mind.

The Family Collie

Whether male or female, the Collie's natural curiosity will cause it to put its long nose in all your projects, inside or out. Both sexes take responsibility for their people family very seriously. While not aggressive in temperament, they seem always to be aware of their surroundings and they like things to be in good order. A yard full of playing children will be well cared for under the watchful eye of the family Collie.

Variety of Coats and Colors

In Collies there are two coat varieties and four recognized colors.

Whether male or female, both make an excellent companion.

Rough coat and Smooth coat denote the length of coat on a Collie, rough being longer and fuller and the most common, and smooth indicating a short-hair coat.

Colors: Both varieties of coats come in one of the four colors.

✔ The most common is sable or sable and white. This color encompasses all shades of brown from deep mahogany to light gold.

✔ The tri-color is black with white and tan markings.

✔ Blue merle is one of the least commonly seen colors but it is growing in popularity. Primarily light or dark gray with shades of black throughout the coat, this color is one of the most challenging patterns to achieve. It has been said that there are not two blue merles the same in coat color patterns.

✔ Another coat color more rarely seen is the white. White-coated Collies have either sable, tri-color, or blue merle-colored heads. The body coat is white, usually with some spots on the body that are the same color as those on the head.

Collar: Almost all Collies have a white collar or at least a partial white collar—white on the chest, some white on the legs, white paws, and tail tip. Sometimes a white blaze on the face, which may or may not disappear as the dog grows older, is present.

Breeding for a particular coat color is a genetic science and must be studied carefully to obtain the correct results.

Looking at a litter of puppies with two or more coat colors in evidence can be confusing especially if you are not acquainted with the various colors. A litter may have both smooth and rough varieties; the breeder will quickly point out the difference. Very young pups do not always have a sufficient amount of coat to easily determine which is which. No matter what color or variety you choose, a litter of Collie puppies is a sight you will long remember.

Selecting the Right One

Now that you know a Collie is the dog for you, and you have located a kennel or breeder with a litter for you to look at, and are armed with some knowledge about the breed, the selection process begins. Keep in mind that if you do not see just what you like or for any reason have doubts about the breeder or person with whom you are dealing, look further. While all puppies are appealing, you must feel satisfied in your own mind that this is the one for you.

═══ T I P ═══

Nutritional Requirements

Dogs' nutritional requirements vary. Their basic needs depend largely on size, activity, and metabolism.

Choosing an outgoing puppy, one that comes to you out of curiosity, one that seems confident with littermates as well as alone, should indicate a secure and happy pup. A young pup with bright eyes, healthy-looking coat, and a good weight will tell you that it is off to a fine start. Do not buy a puppy until it

Color should be of no consequence in choosing your puppy.

is at least eight weeks old; puppies are not ready to make the social adjustment needed to leave their siblings before that age.

Most reputable breeders want good and loving homes for their puppies. A lot of thought, work, and care have gone into these animals. Even though you have a list of questions for the seller, don't be surprised if he or she also has some questions about you.

Questions to the Seller

When the initial contact is made, a few questions from you are appropriate:
✔ What are the ages and sex of the puppies?
✔ How many pups are in the litter?
✔ Are both the sire and dam purebred and/or registered with the American Kennel Club?

The tri-color Collie is black with white and tan markings.

(A registered dog means only that it is purebred, not that it is in any way endorsed by the American Kennel Club.)
✔ Can you see one or both of the parents? If not, why not?
✔ What is the general health and longevity of relatives behind the parents? You should follow with these pertinent queries:
✔ Have the pups received any inoculations?
✔ Have they been wormed or tested for worms?
✔ Have the eyes been checked by a qualified canine ophthalmologist for Collie eye problems (see page 44)?

Price: Price may or may not be discussed at this time. If you know how much you are willing to pay, this is the time to find out if these puppies fit into your budget.

Older puppies: If you are inquiring about an older puppy or a grown dog, the same questions with some modifications would apply. For instance, you might ask why this Collie has not already been sold, or whether the dog has had some training to enable it to become a good family member, such as housetraining and walking with a leash. Often, a puppy is kept by the breeder to watch as a show prospect, but not every puppy grows up to be a show dog or one suitable for breeding. These dogs are often beautiful examples of the breed but for various reasons are not acceptable for show or breeding.

When you are satisfied with the answers to your questions, make an appointment to visit the seller. Be prepared to spend some time looking at the litter, finding out what to expect if you decide to purchase one from this litter.

The Paper Trail

The puppy is yours! If you have purchased a registered AKC Collie puppy, there will be papers to obtain and sign. The breeder will have already registered the puppy as part of a litter resulting from the mating of two pure-bred registered Collies.

Pedigree Form

The seller should provide you with a pedigree form showing the lineage of your puppy with the names of the Collies in its family. This is not a legal document but should be signed by the breeder as being accurate.

Medical Record

A medical record showing dates of inoculations, fecal examinations and results, along with the eye examination report and name of the canine ophthalmologist and veterinarian used should be given to you at the time of purchase. You may certainly ask for this information to be given in writing.

Diets

Since puppies have special needs and requirements regarding their diets, a feeding schedule noting the names of puppy foods, supplements, and amounts to feed are often supplied to the buyer to avoid tummy upsets for the first few days. Ask if the seller will guarantee the health of your puppy for 24 hours—until you can get to your own veterinarian for a checkup. Most sellers are glad to do this but be reasonable about the length of time you request. After all, sellers have no control over the puppy once it leaves their yard. Papers and puppy in hand, a new, wonderful adventure awaits you.

TIP

Shedding

Shedding in both the rough- and smooth-coated Collie occurs once or twice a year. Males usually shed within two or three months after their birthday. Females tend to shed shortly after the end of their season if they have not been spayed. When the hair is noticeably loose, you will see the undercoat loosening or coming out. A warm bath is in order. Daily brushing and combing will help complete this cycle and encourage new coat growth. Shedding will take about three weeks, and approximately six to ten weeks for the new coat replacement. The Collie coat protects against heat as well as cold and should not be cut or shaved except for medical reasons.

Good breeders want loving homes for their puppies.

PUPPY CARE

Most Collie owners enjoy the companionship of their dogs living as indoor pets. A close and lasting relationship between a Collie and its family is formed very quickly. A Collie adapts easily to its role as a household member and seems to need and enjoy this position.

First Days Home

Being prepared to transport your puppy home will make the move easier.

1. If you have a dog carrier, put shredded newspaper in the bottom, along with a bath towel or small blanket. Be sure the carrier is well ventilated.

2. Place the puppy gently into the carrier, reassuring it with a calm voice. The puppy may protest for a few minutes, but if the ride home is relatively smooth, it may fall asleep.

3. Holding the puppy on your lap or close to your side, if you do not have a carrier, will keep it from moving around or falling.

4. The unfamiliar motion of the car could upset its stomach. Place a towel beneath it and keep paper towels handy.

Upon arrival, put the puppy on the ground to relieve itself. Keep a watchful eye, as this will

Puppies need their littermates for at least eight weeks.

take several minutes while it sniffs the new territory.

Before bringing your puppy home, you should decide where it will sleep and spend time when unsupervised. Giving the puppy the run of the house is bewildering for a young dog.

Indoor pen: An indoor pen where the puppy will feel secure will make a safe environment and provide a quiet refuge. Put plenty of newspaper on the floor and be sure the puppy's sleeping area is free from drafts. A few toys of its own and a chew-proof bed will make the new quarters complete.

Baby gates: As it grows and learns house manners, its confinement will be less and less. Putting baby gates across doorways is a good method to contain an older puppy. Discourage chewing on the gate.

Toys

Puppies and older dogs should have their own toys. Small chew toys at first, then hard

First days home can be confusing to any dog.

rubber and flavored rawhide bones are recommended. Be careful of stuffed toys that can be ripped apart, as the pieces can be swallowed. Check "squeakie" toys to be sure the "squeaker" cannot be dislodged. Most Collies love to retrieve. Throwing a hard rubber ball a few feet away and encouraging the puppy to bring it back is a great game as well as one of the first learning experiences.

Getting Acquainted

Give your puppy time to become acquainted. Too much playing and holding will only confuse a young dog. At first, it may not be as playful or outgoing as it seemed to be with its littermates, but try to realize that everything is strange to it and that the safety and protection it felt in its other surroundings are no longer there. Gaining the puppy's confidence can best be done if it is treated gently and spoken to in a calm and friendly tone. Loud noises and sudden movements, grabbing at it, and teasing will only frighten the puppy.

Lifting

Do not lift your puppy by the scruff of the neck or by its front, letting the back legs dangle. Instead, teach everyone in the household to pick the puppy up by putting one hand under the chest and the other under the hindquarters. Young children should be encouraged to sit on the floor before picking up a puppy in order to keep the puppy from being dropped and

Puppies should have a good supply of their own toys.

perhaps suffering permanent injury. Tail pulling, squeezing, and other forms of rough play should be discouraged immediately! A live animal is *not* a plaything but can become a lifelong friend once you have won its confidence.

Sleep

Like babies, all puppies need a great deal of sleep. Keeping a schedule for eating, playtime, and sleep helps the puppy know what is to be expected and in a very short time it will know how to act accordingly.

The first few nights your puppy may not want to be left alone and will cry for attention. Leaving a radio on low, a clock ticking, or giving it a stuffed toy (without buttons or hair to be pulled off and swallowed) can sometimes offer comfort. Putting a warm hot water bottle wrapped in a blanket in with the puppy may help for the first few nights but these props should not be used for a long period. Try not to go to your crying puppy more than once or twice; then stay only a brief time, reassuring it with a quiet and gentle voice. Leave the room immediately. The crying will eventually stop as the puppy becomes secure in its new surroundings—and peaceful nights will return.

Feeding Your Puppy

Your puppy should have its own food and water bowls. The feeding dish should be round, made of stainless steel for easy cleaning, and big enough to accommodate larger amounts of food as the puppy grows. The water bowl needs to be heavy or weighted so it cannot be pushed around or knocked over. Collie puppies like to put their paws in water to play. Keeping water in something deep enough will discourage this

---

TIP

Children and Collies

Toddlers through teens can be given appropriate responsibilities in caring for the family Collie. This will provide children a feeling of accomplishment, teach them patience, and generally contribute toward their emotional growth.

---

play and help to keep your floor from being flooded. Have fresh water available at all times, keeping it in the same place so your puppy will know where to find it.

Missed meals: Feeding should be done at approximately the same time every day and in the same place. If you are unable to feed your puppy on schedule, ask a neighbor or friend to

Speaking in a calm and friendly tone will gain your puppy's confidence.

Remember how fast puppies grow. Make necessary adjustments for living and sleeping space.

help you out. Infrequent feeding or missing meals can cause nutritional imbalance and be detrimental to the puppy's overall health. Do not try to make up for a missed meal. Small puppies have small tummies and cannot be expected to take in more food than their usual ration at any one time. If feeding a very young puppy is impossible for someone in the household to attend to, perhaps an older puppy or a grown Collie would be more suitable.

Consistent repetition will help teach your puppy when it is time to eat. Creating good eating habits at a young age will be a pattern you will want to establish early; these habits remain with the dog the rest of its life.

How Often?

Puppies have their fastest growth rate during the first six months of life. For this reason good nutrition is very important, and will influence its health and well-being as an adult dog. An eight-week-old puppy needs four meals a day—early morning, noon, early evening, and before bedtime. Not all of these meals will necessarily be the same size. The morning and evening meals will be the largest; the noon and late evening will be less. By the twelfth week, or at three months of age, three meals a day is usually sufficient. From six months to a year, two meals—morning and afternoon—should be offered.

Good nutrition is essential at all stages of life.

Introducing New Food

If you have been given a feeding schedule and names of food used by the breeder, it is wise to follow the same routine as closely as possible with the brands of food your puppy has been accustomed to. After a few days you may wish to change brands. Take care to introduce new food slowly by adding a small amount once or twice a day and by adding a bit more each time until the former brand is completely replaced. Remember a sudden change in diet may cause an upset at any age; therefore, it is important to proceed slowly. Watching stool composition each day will help to determine if the new food agrees with your puppy. A loose stool for more than one day indicates a need to start again with less of the new food or perhaps another brand.

Do not try to save money on dog food. There are many good brands on the market that will fulfill your puppy's needs. Ask your veterinarian for advice if you are unfamiliar with a high-quality food.

Doghouses

Collies seem to enjoy cold weather but a puppy under the age of four months should not be left outside for long periods of time. If the dog is to live outside, it should have a draft-free, well-insulated doghouse that is raised off the ground and waterproof. There are many well-constructed houses that can be purchased from pet supply stores or lumberyards, or you can build one yourself. The house should be large enough for the dog to turn around in but small enough for its body to heat it. Filling the house

Keep a schedule for eating,
playtime, and sleep.

TIP

The Value of Crates

Just as parents use playpens or cribs to confine young children when they are unsupervised, crates or cages have been used for years by professional breeders and pet owners.

with straw in the winter and tacking up a piece of burlap across the doorway will help keep out the wind. Be sure to get rid of the bedding in the spring to avoid fleas and ticks. Shade is an important consideration in the summer. As much as dogs like the cooler weather in the fall and winter, they do not like nor do well in extreme heat. Avoiding weather extremes in any season is advisable. Sleeping inside during the daytime in winter, then putting your Collie out for the night is liable to make it ill. And remember—free access to fresh water is essential at all times.

House-training

Whether your puppy lives inside the house with the family or is to be an outside dog, some basic training will be in order. It is never too early to begin house-training. In fact, this training should begin the very first day home. Collies by nature are clean dogs and will not soil their living quarters, if at all possible. Allowing the puppy to go outside frequently is necessary to complete the training quickly. It is not uncommon for a Collie puppy to be house-trained within a week if a routine is faithfully followed.

For the first several weeks or so, take the puppy outside first thing in the morning. The last outing should be as late as possible until the puppy is able to control its bladder for long periods of time.

Good habits remain with your Collie a lifetime.

Leaving newspaper in its confined area for a few days to catch any accidents will be necessary. As it learns to use the outdoors to relieve itself, you will be able to take up the papers during the day as long as there is someone at home to take the puppy outside. When the nighttime papers remain dry, begin to take those away, too. Your puppy will try to tell you when it needs to go out by putting its nose to the floor and moving about quickly, sometimes in circles. The puppy will appear distracted, anxious, and may whine or cry. That is the time to pick it up and carry it outside. Taking the puppy to the same place each time will allow it

Puppy Training at a Glance

Eating at mealtime	Offer food at the same time each day. Allow 15 or 20 minutes for the puppy to complete its meal. Throw away the uneaten portion. Learn to feed the correct amount of food by how much the puppy consumes at each meal. Keep treats to minimum; use only when training.
Sleeping	Small puppies require a lot of rest and should be given a safe place to sleep. Give reassurance for the first few nights, along with a ticking clock or radio left on low and perhaps a warm hot water bottle wrapped securely in a towel.
Come when called	Sit down and pat the floor to get the puppy's attention. Call its name followed by *"Come."* Use an excited tone of voice. Reward the puppy when it comes to you. Retrieving a ball or playing hide and seek are other games used to teach the *"Come"* command.
Sit when ordered	This command is taught after the puppy knows how to come on command. Say *"Sit"* each time while very gently pushing down on its rear. Each time the puppy completes this command, praise and a treat will enforce its confidence to do it again.
Walking on leash	Use a nylon leash with a well-fitting lightweight leather collar and let the puppy drag it around the house, with supervision, for a few minutes at a time. After a few times take the puppy outside and let it lead you around for the first outings. With the leash in one hand and a squeaky toy or treat in the other, coax the puppy into following you. Lots of praise will teach your puppy to look forward to trips on the leash.
House-training	Taking the puppy outside to the same place each time to "potty," and a watchful eye for signs indicating that the puppy needs to go will get the training accomplished within a week or so.

to get the scent of the previous time and encourage it to urinate or move its bowels. Lots of praise, a pat to say, *"Good puppy,"* and *"Good job"* expresses your pleasure, and each time it will be more eager for your approval.

A word of caution: Initially, puppies find carpet an almost irresistible target. Keeping the dog in the kitchen or on flooring that can be easily cleaned if an accident occurs will avoid scoldings and hurt feelings for the young dog.

Of course, puppies need to be reprimanded for wrongdoings and should be told in a firm voice how displeased you are. Using the same words each time, either for praise or to scold, will tell it right away how you feel. Consistently sending the right signals will teach it quickly what you expect.

Confining Your Puppy in the Yard

Having a fenced yard or a fenced play area for your puppy is an important consideration as a responsible owner, not only for the safety of your Collie, but as a considerate neighbor as well. Allowing your Collie to run loose only invites trouble and sometimes unfortunate accidents resulting in death. In most areas today, any dog wandering unattended and not on a leash will be picked up by the local authorities and taken to a shelter. If you are lucky enough to find your dog there, you will have to pay a hefty fine. A Collie puppy is an

A fenced play area is important for the safety of your Collie and will help prevent unfortunate accidents.

irresistible sight and a puppy found outside alone is sure to be stolen. Dognapping is a serious problem in this country. Many dogs are stolen out of the owners' yards and transported across state lines to other communities for resale through pet stores, while others are sold for research purposes. These sad facts are not meant to frighten you as an owner but to educate and make you aware of the dangers.

Confining Your Puppy Within the House

If you leave your puppy alone in the house without being confined, you are courting disaster. All puppies chew. They look for new things to play with, not knowing that your favorite table or chair leg does not belong to them. Scatter

Early leash training will enable your Collie to accompany you on wonderful outings.

rugs, drapery hems, your most expensive shoes, or your children's video games all seem like toys to an inquisitive and investigating puppy.

Boredom from being alone will cause dogs to bark, creating a problem that is hard to break. Leaving your dog—puppy or grown—alone for long periods of time is not a good idea. Collies are social animals and require people in their lives. If you must be away and there is not a family member able to check on your Collie, investigate the possibility of a dog walker or a person who will come to the house a few times during the day to feed and let your dog outside for a brief period of play.

Walking on a Leash

Taking your puppy with you whenever possible will enable it to feel confident and calm, no matter what comes along. Early leash training, and learning a few simple commands makes

TIP

Basic Commands

A few basic commands can be taught to a young puppy but it is better to wait a few months for more formalized training. The attention span of a young dog is not very long so the lessons must be short.

trips with you fun. Teaching a young puppy to walk on a leash takes only a few lessons.

✔ Start by putting a light collar around its neck.

✔ Pay particular attention to the fit of the collar. You will need to replace it several times as the dog grows.

✔ When the puppy seems comfortable wearing the collar, snap on a lightweight leash and let it drag the leash along behind it. This exercise should be done in the house, under supervision, for only a few minutes at a time.

✔ After a few days, try this outside. You must stay with the dog so that the leash does not become entangled.

✔ Now pick up the leash, letting the puppy lead you around.

Choke chain on smooth-coated Collie.

✔ Lots of praise and petting will let your puppy know that it is doing a good thing. Before long, it will know when it sees the collar and leash in your hand that it will be going out with you and you will be greeted with excitement and anticipation.

The Car

Riding in the car should be something your Collie does with ease. Learning to lie down and remain quiet while traveling is another early lesson to be taught. This can be done with two people, one working with the puppy while the other is driving. Even though the puppy is still small, it will eventually grow into a big dog. For this reason, it must be taught to ride in the backseat. If you have room, putting your dog in a wire cage is the safest way to travel. Don't be surprised if at first the puppy drools excessively or becomes upset. Taking short trips at the

Jumping, excessive barking, and rough play should be discouraged starting at a young age.

beginning will accustom it to the motion of the car and it should quickly learn to travel well.

Once your puppy has learned to walk along with you and can ride in the car, introducing it to other people and places will be an easy thing to accomplish.

Learning to Behave Well

By the time the puppy reaches six months of age, and you have been consistent with your training, it should know how to eat at meal-time, sleep quietly at night, come when its name is called, walk on the leash, ride in the car, and know the meaning of the word *"No."* Excessive barking, jumping up on people, rough play, such as hand biting or pulling on trouser legs, should have been discouraged.

Your Collie should know the difference between your belongings and its toys. It is still a young dog and will continue to do puppy things, but by now it understands when you are pleased and when it has done something wrong.

Visiting the Veterinarian

One of the first trips you take with your puppy should be to the veterinarian. The doctor will give your new puppy a thorough examination and put it on a schedule for a series of puppy shots and rabies inoculations.

It is important to stay on the schedule of shots your veterinarian gives you. He or she is vaccinating your puppy against diseases that are life-threatening and providing protection that the puppy's immune system cannot handle.
✔ If the seller has given you a health record, be sure to take it with you. Depending upon the age of your puppy, it may have already had some of its shots and your veterinarian will need this information. This is also a good time to ask questions about diet, diet supplements, and general health care.
✔ Ask about microchipping or tatooing, now routinely offered to identify your pet if lost.
✔ When you call to make an appointment, the receptionist will probably ask you to bring a stool sample to be tested for parasites, commonly called worms.
✔ Be sure to discuss heartworm prevention. Collies are acutely sensitive to the drug Ivermectin with a potentially fatal toxic reaction.
✔ Whether or not you have purchased your puppy on a spay or neutering contract, your first visit to the veterinarian is a good time to discuss these procedures. The need to control pet over-population caused by indiscriminate breeding is an important consideration and one you must address. Aside from the population issue, there are many benefits associated with early spaying or neutering. Decreasing the incidence of uterine infection, mammary and testicular tumors, of which an alarming number have been found to be cancerous, is just one of the benefits.

If you don't know a veterinarian, before you bring your new puppy home, check with friends who already own dogs for recommendations or call local breeders for suggestions.

CHECKLIST

Choosing a Veterinarian

1. Choosing one who is close to your home is helpful, but should not be the only determining factor.

2. The office should be clean and free from odors.

3. The doctor and staff should be friendly and polite, ready to answer questions freely and to discuss treatments in an easy-to-understand manner.

4. Do not hesitate to ask about fees and methods of payment.

5. Also ask about emergency hours. For some reason, most critical problems arise after office hours, on holidays, or on weekends.

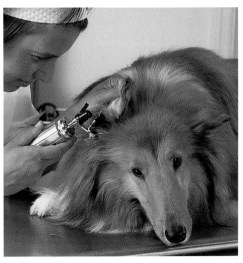

Make a list of questions to ask your veterinarian.

The Collie coat is described as its "crowning glory"; therefore, proper care from the dog's owner is not only beneficial but necessary. Grooming your Collie is easier than perhaps it may first appear. A thorough brushing once a week takes care of the thickest coat and encourages the natural oils to repel odor, dirt, and matting.

Tools

The most commonly used tool is the pin brush, a wood or plastic long-handled brush with stainless steel pins that will get through the densest coat. Be sure the pins are not so stiff as to break the hair. A pair of small sharp scissors, a metal comb, nail cutters, and a plastic spray bottle will help you keep your Collie looking and feeling good.

Elevating Your Dog

Teaching your Collie to stand quietly on a sturdy grooming table will make your weekly examination and brushing much easier. A daily check for fleas and ticks in summer is especially important.

Check the Inside of the Ears

Excess dirt or wax should be carefully wiped away by using an ear cleaning solution made for dogs. Dab lightly around the inside with a cotton ball. If no problem is apparent, cleaning need be done only on a monthly basis.

Check the Eyes

The eyes should be bright and clear without any discharge. Any matter in or around the eyes should be gently wiped away with warm water. Start at the inside

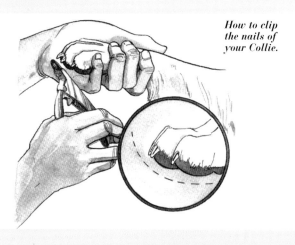

How to clip the nails of your Collie.

corner and work out. The appearance of pus or excessive discharge indicates a probable infection and a call to the veterinarian is in order.

The Mouth

A look inside the mouth for tooth tartar buildup or dental problems is recommended. This examination is important for a puppy, too, especially when baby teeth are loosening and permanent teeth are beginning to appear. Watch for correct alignment to ensure proper chewing. Offering your Collie hard bones (such as Milk Bones) and rawhide chews help keep the teeth clean. It is now widely accepted that regularly brushing the dog's teeth with a toothpaste or dental solution especially manufactured for dogs has proved effective.

Feet and Nails

The feet and nails should be trimmed about once a month. Ask your veterinarian or a professional groomer to show you how to use the clippers. Dogs don't particularly like to have their feet fussed with, so learning the correct way from the beginning will save time and stress.

Clipping the nails allows the dog to walk more comfortably. Cutting the hair around the pads on the bottom of the feet keeps mud and snow from caking between the toes and again adds comfort in walking.

Matting

The best way to remove a mat is to carefully cut it away, then comb through the area to be sure that no tangles remain. Sometimes rubbing a bit of baby powder into the mat and gently working the area with your fingers and a comb will loosen it enough for you to thoroughly comb it out.

Bathing

Bathing a Collie several times a year is usually adequate to maintain its coat. If you are exhibiting at dog shows or other events, more frequent washing will be necessary, but for general maintenance, unless something unusual occurs, occasional bathing and weekly brushing will be enough. Because of the breed's double coat—soft, close fur next to the skin with harsher and longer hair on top—it is important to use enough warm water to get the hair wet to the skin. Using a mild dog shampoo, lather the coat from the skin outward, being careful not to get soap in the eyes or ears. Rinsing shampoo from the hair is as important as the washing. Leaving soap residue in the coat or on the skin will make the hair dull and cause the skin to be dry and itchy. Towel dry the dog, then let it shake as much water as possible from it, and towel dry again. Follow by gently brushing all over to keep mats from forming.

Warning: Do not use a flea and/or tick shampoo if you are using one of the widely available flea and tick preventives. A toxic reaction may occur.

Drying: Bathing on a warm day will allow your Collie to dry naturally without becoming chilled. In cool or cold weather, keep it inside until dry. Using a hair dryer turned on the warm setting

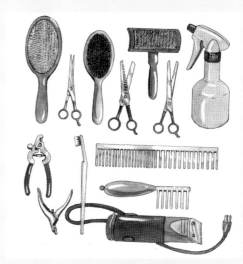

A complete selection of grooming tools for your pet.

will help dry the dog more quickly. Keep the dog away from drafts until it is dry.

Brushing

Brushing your Collie can be done easily and quickly after you have practiced a few times. Use a plastic spray bottle (similar to the bottle used for misting plants) filled with water to mist the whole coat. Take your pin brush and begin just behind the ears, brushing the hair forward. Using this method will enable the natural oils in the hair follicles to be brought to the hairtips, giving the coat a shiny appearance.

As you spray and brush, the coat will stand up. After brushing the whole coat in this manner, gently brush the hair in a downward motion. The coat will now appear in its natural state. Don't forget the chest and tail. If the white parts on feet and legs are a bit dull, mist the area and rub cornstarch or baby powder into and against the hair. When the white parts of the coat are dry, remove the excess powder by brushing.

GROWING UP

Collies are by instinct herding dogs—they want to work, to have a job. As they grow older, their sense of pleasing their owner and trying to anticipate his or her wishes or moods becomes very evident.

Training

Even though a Collie's herding ability and eagerness to take on responsibilities around the home seem a natural part of its makeup, this eagerness does not always carry over into formalized obedience training.

Collies take harsh correction very personally. They don't have to be told many times that they have done or are doing something displeasing to you. Hitting a Collie with your hand, or worse with a rolled-up newspaper, in order to punish it for a misdeed, will only give you an unhappy and reluctant dog. The Collie's natural sweet and gentle nature seem to make it almost impossible for it to understand or accept angry and imprudent conduct. While they are quick to forgive your anger, they will not respond to your training with the happiness and eagerness you would like to

Be sure you are ready for a long-term commitment to care for and love this deserving breed.

see. This does not mean, however, that firmness and reprimands are not in order while teaching your dog. Once the lesson has been learned, lavish praise and a hug will imprint the message in a way that will be rewarding to you both.

Like all dogs, Collies are also pack animals. Their heritage dictates there must be leaders and followers. All it has learned as an infant puppy, it learned from its dam. Now that it is in your care, it must learn that you are the leader. Rarely does a Collie challenge the authority of a human being. The exceptions would of course include imminent danger to its family and, in some cases, threats to its territory. Establishing yourself as a pack leader, or Alpha, is an important step early in the dog's training.

When to Begin

Other than some very basic training referred to earlier, obedience training should begin at about six months of age. If, after a few lessons,

The Collie is equally at home in the city or the country.

you see that the dog is reluctant or unhappy, it might be wise to put them off for a while.

Obedience training not only gives you a well-behaved Collie, but adds a measure of self-confidence to the dog. A well-trained dog is ready for all kinds of work around the home as well as in the community.

The Importance of Exercise

An important factor in the health and well-being of your Collie is exercise. A dog that has exercise on a daily basis will have less pent-up energy that can lead to misbehavior.

You should be part of your dog's play and exercise program. Not only will you both become healthier, but you will strengthen a growing emotional bond that will last throughout the years.

Types of Exercise

Very young puppies should not be encouraged to take long jogging runs or to jump. Putting too much stress on growing and

Professional training ensures satisfactory results.

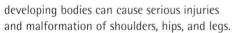

A morning and evening exercise program keep you and your Collie in good health.

developing bodies can cause serious injuries and malformation of shoulders, hips, and legs.

Exercise and strenuous activities should be curtailed in very hot or humid weather; try to get out with your dog very early in the morning, even before the sun is up, for a walk or a game of chase and fetch. In this day of fitness awareness, a two- or three-mile walk with your Collie should be just the thing to get your day off to a good start.

Playing alone: A Collie will play for a long time chasing after a ball or stick, happily returning it to you for another chance to run for it. Some have become quite proficient with a

TIP

Keeping Watch

When we call our Collies in for the night, one dog has taken it upon himself to make sure that all are accounted for. Normally, he is the first one to come to the door, then turns to wait for the rest to appear. If one or more have stopped along the way, for whatever reason, he will return to the runs or paddock and round up the late comer. Only when all have arrived is he content to go into his bed. Giving us a look that tells us he is pleased with himself and his self-appointed task, he settles down for his rest.

A stately tri-color Rough Collie displays its glorious white collar, ruff, and coat.

Frisbee as well. Putting your dog out in the backyard by itself is not exercise unless there is another dog to play with. Even then, you will want to keep an eye on the play to be sure one is not so dominant over the other as to cause a threat of safety.

Routine

When dogs are left alone all day, it is doubly important that they have a routine exercise program. Routine is the key word here—dogs of all ages thrive on routine. Physical and mental exercise keep the body and mind busy. Keeping up with your dog's learned obedience commands is an excellent way to challenge its mind. Ask it to *sit* before it eats or is given a treat, when you attach the leash, or before you throw a ball. Vary the situations with the *down, stay* command. Call the dog to you using its name several times throughout the play period, and use the *heel* command when walking or running.

Dog Walkers

It can also be helpful to hire a dog walker to come in the middle of the day to exercise the dog. Be sure the person is reliable and will come at approximately the same time every day. This short break in the day does not take the place of a morning exercise program or an evening jaunt but should be considered an addition to other activities.

A well-groomed Collie is certain to attract favorable attention.

Classes

An organized training class is usually the most satisfactory method used for obedience training. The instructors are professional trainers and deal with all kinds of dogs and dog-related problems.

Training at Home

Training your Collie at home on an informal basis can also be effective. Teaching the basic commands of *sit, down, stay,* and *heel* may be taught without any formal training when you are consistent in your methods and with your time. If your puppy can sit on command, come when it is called, and respond appropriately to the word *"No,"* you are well on your way. Getting its attention and maintaining eye contact are very important. Creating a pleasant learning atmosphere while remaining serious during train-

Receiving the command heel.

The stay command is the last of the basic orders.

ing lets the dog know that this is not playtime but something you want it to do when asked.

Be sure to use the same words each time for the commands you are teaching. Teach the other members in the household which words you are using for commands. There are books and manuals in the library, bookstore, or pet supply outlet to help you learn these commands and methods.

Heel

After your Collie has reached the age of six months and is able to sit on command and walk along on the leash, the command *heel* is the next lesson. Heeling keeps the dog walking beside you, close to your left leg, without pulling on the leash.

The *heel* command requires the use of a stainless steel

chain collar, referred to as a choke chain. They come in various lengths, but should not be more than 4 inches (10 cm) longer than the fit around the dog's neck. There is a ring on both ends of the collar. When putting this collar on your dog, you must first double part of the chain through one of the rings to form a sort of noose. As you face your dog, slip the chain over its head so that the top of the chain connected to the free ring is resting on top of the neck, not underneath the chin. Snap a leather leash on the free ring. As you pull up on the leash, the collar should close quickly and release again as pressure is released. Be sure the chain is on the dog correctly or it will not release smoothly and could cause the dog to choke. This type of collar is designed for two purposes—it combines comfort for the dog, assuming it fits properly, and offers control for the handler.

✔ To begin the lesson, your Collie should be in the sitting position on your left side looking straight ahead.

✔ Place the end of the leash in your right hand and pass the rest of it across your body, holding the remainder in your left hand a few inches above his neck.

OBEDIENCE

✔ Your left hand will be used to supply the corrective action.

✔ As you step off on your left foot, give a slight upward jerk on the leash and the command *heel.*

✔ As the dog begins to move out in front of you, give another quick jerking motion using the word *heel* again.

✔ Keep your voice firm and repeat this exercise as often as needed until your Collie is walking beside you without exerting pressure on the leash.

✔ When you come to a stop, tell your dog *"Sit."* Remember to release the pressure quickly as the commands are obeyed and say *"Good dog"* as it begins to learn this lesson. As always, give a lot of praise when the session has ended.

Training is like a game for your dog. It will be eager to please you but is likely to become bored if it goes on too long. Two or three five-minute lessons will be enough for a few days, then you can expand it into two ten-minute lessons. End each lesson with some playtime after removing the choke collar and leash.

Down

When the *heel* command has been learned and is working well, you can proceed to the command *down.*

As a rule, dogs are not comfortable sitting for long periods of time. Therefore, the command *down,* meaning to lie down, is a good lesson to teach. The easiest way to get the dog down is to first have it in a sitting position. While pulling the leash in a downward motion with your right hand, push firmly on its back at about the shoulder level, giving the command *down.* It should go into the correct position. Praise it loudly.

Another method is to put the dog in the sitting position at your side. Get down on one knee with your left hand against the dog's

*Understanding the **down** command.*

shoulder. Using your right hand, pick the dog's left foot off the ground, while pressure from your left hand forces the dog down sideways. Do this at the same time you are saying *"Down."* Or, you may have the dog sit while you gently slide its front feet forward until it is in the *down* position. Again, issue the command in a firm voice—*"Down."* However you accomplish this task, praising your dog each time it completes the procedure is the reward it will be expecting.

Stay

This command can be done after your dog has mastered the *sit* and *down* lessons. While it is in one of these positions, hold the leash in your right hand and move a few feet away, while saying *"Sit," "Stay,"* or *"Down-Stay."* When it begins to move or starts to get up, return to it quickly and start again with *sit* or *down,* and then repeating *"Stay"* while moving away.

This exercise will take more time for the dog to learn, but as it begins to stay in place for a few more seconds each time, you can move farther away until you are at the end of the leash.

HEALTH

Common sense is your best guide to evaluating your Collie's health or when to call the veterinarian. When you notice a deviation in its usual daily pattern, take a few minutes to determine whether or not there is a problem.

When to Call the Veterinarian

Use your common sense when you notice any of the following:

Diarrhea: All dogs have occasionally loose stools. Usually it is due to a change in diet. If the condition becomes acute and frequent, if the stool is passed as liquid, or if you see blood, call the veterinarian.

Loss of appetite: If the dog is normally a good eater and its appetite goes off for a couple of days, it should be examined for an abscessed tooth, or for internal problems.

Ears: Excessive scratching or digging around its ears, holding its head to one side, or shaking its head from time to time indicates a possible

Always check with your veterinarian if you think there's a problem with your Collie's health.

ear infection and will need the attention of the veterinarian.

Choking: Choking or difficulty swallowing is an obvious symptom of a problem in the throat. Pry apart the jaws and look in the mouth for any foreign objects. If you find nothing there, an appointment with the veterinarian for further evaluation is necessary. Persistent coughing can be due to diseases of the throat and respiratory system or to parasites and should be investigated.

Coat: If your Collie's coat is not as shiny as usual, perhaps thinning and dry, if its skin appears flaky and it is losing weight, consult your veterinarian, who will do a fecal examination for internal parasites. Specific patches of hair loss, exposing red or inflamed skin, may indicate mange. This can be treated by your veterinarian with dips and prescription ointments.

Other signs: Prolonged limping, vomiting, fever, excessive intake of water, frequent urination, or wincing in pain when touched are all

Collie puppies should have their eyes examined by a qualified canine ophthalmologist.

reasons to call the veterinarian. Collies are almost always stoic, rarely whimpering or crying out when in pain. As a result, it is important to be alert to changes in behavior and overall health.

In case of an emergency, it is a good idea to keep an emergency telephone number close at hand for weekends and after office hours.

Collies are normally strong, healthy animals, living to be 11 to 13 years of age with relatively few problems. But like all living creatures, they are subject to diseases and birth defects.

Collie Eye Anomaly

Fortunately, the number of genetic health-related problems found in Collies are few. One genetic or inherited problem most associated with the breed is Collie Eye Anomaly. This condition may be diagnosed as early as six weeks of age and does not vary in severity

as the dog matures. The defect, if slight, does not seem to affect vision, but it is a problem you should discuss with the breeder.

PRA

Another eye disease found in dogs is Progressive Retinal Atrophy (PRA). This disease affects the retina of the eye with a degenerative process that eventually results in blindness. Most Collies do not have PRA. Puppies can be examined as young as eight weeks by a licensed canine ophthalmologist to determine whether or not this condition is present. Conscientious breeding practices and ongoing research by several veterinary schools in the field of canine ophthalmology are making great strides to eliminate these hereditary defects.

All Collie puppies should have their eyes examined by a qualified canine ophthalmologist before purchase.

Other Genetic Diseases

While such conditions as cancer, epilepsy, bloat, and immune system problems are known to occur in the breed, it is still unknown if these conditions are hereditary.

Hip dysplasia is rarely found in Collies.

First Aid

In the case of an accident, a knowledge of first aid may help to save your dog's life. Accidents happen at unexpected times and it is not always possible to reach your veterinarian in an emergency. However, it is important to recognize your own limitations. Your quick action could help your dog before you get help but it may have suffered extensive internal injuries (from a fall or from being struck by a car) and not show any signs of it for a day or so afterwards until it may suddenly begin to hemorrhage. Therefore, no matter how minor you feel the emergency is, it is always best to follow the incident with a visit to the veterinarian for a thorough examination.

Using common sense is the best way to deal with an emergency. While a knowledge of first aid is important for you and your Collie, not having to put this knowledge to the test is far more gratifying. As in all medical situations requiring fast action, the cardinal rule is not to panic but to remain calm and think about what you are doing. If there is time, call someone for assistance—the adage that two heads are better than one is often true. Keeping your dog safe from harm is as much your duty as it is the dog's to protect you—and never leave your dog in someone else's care without providing emergency phone numbers for your veterinarian as well as yourself.

First Aid Kit

It is helpful to keep emergency supplies handy. Gather these supplies soon after your Collie comes home. Be sure to label the container carefully and keep track of the contents so that medications with expiration dates are kept updated. Some of the items you will need are

✔ digital thermometer
✔ 3 × 3-inch (7.6-cm) and 4 × 4-inch (10-cm) sterile gauze pads
✔ gauze bandage, 2-inch (5-cm) and 3-inch (7.6-cm) sizes
✔ self-adhesive bandage roll
✔ cotton pads, balls, and swabs
✔ adhesive tape
✔ hydrogen peroxide for cleansing wounds

Fact of Life

A puppy's fastest growth rate occurs during the first six months of life.

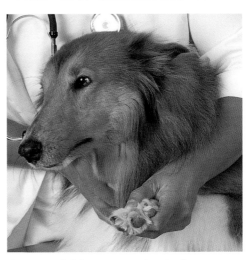

Keep available your veterinarian's emergency telephone number for those after-office hours and weekend crises.

✔ antiseptic for minor cuts
✔ germicidal soap
✔ antibacterial skin cream
✔ blunt-tipped scissors
✔ antidiarrhea preparation, such as Kaopectate.

Ask your veterinarian for other suggestions or comments as to what items to keep on hand.

Temperature: The normal temperature for an adult dog is 100° to 103°F (37.8–39.4°C). The average is 101.3°F (38.3°C).

The normal pulse is 70 to 130 beats per minute at rest. Normal respiration is 10 to 30 breaths per minute at rest.

*Your veterinarian should be the one to
determine the method of treatment.*

Internal bleeding: Internal injuries are not always apparent after an accident, but if the gums are pale gray in color and the dog is weak or prostrate, it may be hemorrhaging internally. Using an improvised stretcher made from a door or a couple of large flat boards fastened together is by far the best method of transporting an injured dog. If neither of these is available to you, use a blanket or large coat, tying knots in each corner. Place strong poles through the knots so that two people can carry the dog to the car. Try not to change the dog's position when sliding it onto a stretcher. Take it to the nearest veterinary clinic; time is *not* on your side.

Bleeding from the nose but no apparent damage to the nostrils may indicate a head injury. If there is bleeding from the mouth, inspect the tongue and inside the mouth for cuts. Even when there is no immediate sign of internal bleeding, an examination after an accident is strongly recommended.

Choking: The sound of a dog choking should bring you to its aid immediately—it may have something caught in its throat. Open the mouth wide by placing one hand on the lower jaw and one hand around the top of the muzzle. Then pry open the jaws and take a look. If you cannot see anything, push your finger into the throat as deeply as possible and rub the surface gently to try and dislodge any small obstruction that might be present. If you cannot determine the cause of the choking, call for veterinarian assistance.

Occasionally, food or a bone can become lodged crosswise in the back of the mouth behind the teeth or between the teeth and outer gums. The dog will open and close its mouth, shake its head, or lower its head and try to get its foot into its mouth to dislodge the cause of the discomfort. Usually it is a simple matter to remove the article but it may require two people to get the job done—one to hold the dog's mouth open and the other to grab the object with the fingers and get it loose. If this approach is unsuccessful, take your Collie to the veterinarian immediately.

Persistent vomiting is an unmistakable symptom of something lodged in the intestinal tract, indicating that the object has gone past the throat. A veterinarian must be the one to decide the method of treatment.

Bone splinters: Collies, like most dogs, have very strong jaws and can splinter a cooked bone in just a few minutes. The splinters then become lodged in the throat or, worse, in the intestine. Once in the intestine, the small sharp pieces of bone can perforate or puncture the intestine wall. Often, a very expensive surgical procedure will be needed to remove the bone fragment. Today, there are plenty of good bone substitutes found in the pet supply stores. A good rawhide bone, knotted at both ends, will offer many hours of chewing and will keep your Collie satisfied and occupied.

Eyes: Cuts and scratches may cause a mild inflammation in your dog's eyes. Consult your veterinarian, who will determine the treatment. Administering salves or ointments without knowing the specific cause of the problem could cause irreparable damage.

Cuts: Most cuts are not severe. A jagged cut or tear that appears deep, or a puncture wound, should be seen by a veterinarian as soon as possible. Both will need to be checked for foreign matter and will no doubt need antibiotic treatment. In the case of an elongated tear or laceration that is unusually deep, stitches will be needed to close the area. Until you can get the dog to the veterinarian, cut the hair away as close to the skin as possible and administer hydrogen peroxide to the wound. If the wound is on the face or legs, place a sterile gauze pad over the site and try to close or keep the area from widening by placing two bandages or adhesive tape in the form of an "X" on top of the gauze pad and attaching it to healthy skin. This probably will not hold very long because of the hair, but it is worth a try. Keep the dog quiet until you receive professional help.

Severe arterial bleeding: Blood from a severed artery will be bright red and flow in spurts, in time with the heartbeat. The blood from a cut vein is darker red and will flow

TIP

Inoculations

Heartworm preventative and Lyme disease should be discussed with your veterinarian. Monthly medication is available to prevent heartworm, but be sure the treatment has been approved for Collies as serious reactions to certain types of drugs (i.e., Ivermectin) have been reported. Inoculations are also available for Lyme disease prevention.

Collies, by nature, are usually stoic with a high pain tolerance.

evenly. To stop the bleeding from an artery, apply pressure between the heart and wound so that as little blood as possible can run out. To stop the bleeding from a cut, apply pressure below the wound. Use a piece of bedsheet, a cotton undershirt, or a nylon stocking as a tourniquet. Place it in the correct position for the type of wound and twist the ends together until the right amount of pressure has been applied to control the bleeding. Remember to release the pressure every ten minutes or so. When the bleeding has been controlled, wash the area with clean water and a soft cloth and cover it with sterile gauze, then with cotton (don't place the cotton directly over the injury), and wrap with a bandage. Be careful not to bandage so tightly as to stop the circulation. Take the Collie to your veterinarian

Collies generally live between 11 and 13 years although some Collies live 14 to 16 years.

promptly, keeping it as quiet as possible while traveling. If someone cannot drive you to the veterinarian, put the dog in a crate to keep it from moving about and reopening the wound.

Shock: The most common forms of shock are caused by heatstroke, burns, or being hit by a car; however, shock may occur after any injury. The dog may be in a state of complete collapse or unusually nervous excitement. The symptoms are a weak pulse and shallow breathing. The eyes appear "glassy" and the gums are usually pale—signs of impending circulation failure. Keep the dog as quiet as possible. Keep loud noises and talk to a minimum.

Never put off taking a sick or injured Collie to the veterinarian.

If the weather is cool, cover the dog with a coat or warm blanket. Try to keep its body warm and at an even temperature.

Heatstroke: Heatstroke occurs when the dog is left exposed to severe heat from the sun and humidity or when left in a parked car or small building where there is insufficient air circulation. Many dogs are found dead every summer, left in parked cars while the owner runs into the store "for just a minute." On an average summer day in a closed car, the temperature can reach an unbearable 160°F (71°C). Your Collie could die within 15 minutes even with your car windows partly open. The heart and lungs can be permanently damaged.

In the case of heatstroke, a dog's temperature is elevated to a dangerous level and its body must be cooled as quickly as possible. Move the dog into the shade if it is outside. Apply ice packs or immerse it in cool water. If neither of these methods is available, use the garden hose to wet it down. Keep the dog as quiet as possible. You should see some improvement in a few minutes. See your veterinarian as soon as possible in case additional treatment is necessary. The dog may need oxygen therapy or intravenous injected fluids.

Burns: In all cases of burn accidents, keep the burned areas as clean as possible until you can get further professional help.

Drowning: All dogs can swim but even the strongest swimmer can drown if it becomes exhausted. Because the Rough Collie carries such a thick and heavy coat, it is at a great disadvantage in the water. Once the hair becomes water-logged, it acts as an additional weight.

The Collie will tire quickly and may need help getting to shore or to dry ground. Your Collie should not be encouraged to swim in a pool. If it should accidentally fall into a steep-sided swimming pool or pond, there is very little place for it to get a good foothold or find an area where it can get out.

Should your Collie get itself into this situation and you need to revive it, the remedy is much like that given to a human being. Before giving artificial respiration, hold your dog up by the hindlegs at the hocks (the area where the upper and lower leg meets) to expel the

excess water out of the lungs. Lay the dog on a flat surface with the right side down, extend the head and neck, and pull the tongue forward. Then push down on the ribcage, releasing the pressure rhythmically every four or five seconds. Another method to use is "mouth-to-nose" respiration. Pull the tongue forward and close the mouth. Seal the lips with your hand. Place your mouth over the dog's nose and blow in steadily for three seconds. The chest will expand. Release to let the air come back out. Keep this up with regularity. As long as there is a heartbeat, there is hope. When your dog begins to show signs of recovery, rub it

Because rough-coated Collies have heavy coats, they are at a great disadvantage in water.

briskly all over with a towel, then wrap it in a coat or blanket to keep it warm while taking it to the veterinarian for further treatment. This experience has caused severe stress on the dog's respiratory system and you will need professional advice on how to take care of it.

Poisoning: Keep household and garden products out of the reach of your dog. Read labels carefully when using any type of insecticides or products used to kill grasses or weeds.

These types of agents can be absorbed into a dog's system through the pads on the feet. Puppies will investigate anything and older dogs may take a liking to a toxic substance such as lethal antifreeze. Prevention is better than emergency treatment and antidotes.

Recognizable symptoms of poisoning are retching and heavy strings of saliva, pain, trembling, staggering, and sometimes convulsions. If you know what your dog has ingested, take a sample to your veterinarian so that the proper antidote can be given.

Most universities or colleges with a veterinary school have poison control centers and are glad to answer your call for help. It is important to correctly identify the cause of the poisoning.

Administering Medicine

If your veterinarian prescribes an oral medication you should know how to administer it yourself.

Liquids: Use the lip pocket method to give liquids to a dog that cannot drink from a dish or that must be forced to take liquid medicine. Hold the dog's head up. Put your fingers in the side of the mouth at the corner, and pull out the lower lip to form a pocket. Pour or spoon the liquid into this pocket, keeping the dog's head up. The liquid will run between the teeth and down the throat so that it swallows it. Stroking the underside of the chin and throat area after the medication has been given will encourage your dog to swallow all of the liquid medicines.

Pills and capsules: Giving your dog a capsule or pill can be a challenge to your resourcefulness. You can try to fool your Collie by placing the pill inside some raw hamburger made into a small meatball, or in some other favorite food to disguise the taste. Some dogs will just eat them as part of their meal when put into their food.

The most common method used is simply to open the dog's mouth by placing one hand under the jaw and one hand across the top of the muzzle, applying a little pressure against the upper teeth and prying the mouth open. Keeping the capsule or pill in the hand with the lower jaw, simply drop it as far back on the top of the dog's tongue toward its throat as possible. Close its mouth immediately and begin stroking the throat to help it swallow. Be sure to watch it for a few moments to be sure it does not spit out the pill. If this occurs, repeat the procedure until the pill is gone. Occasionally, we have had a Collie that would try to hide the pill away in his mouth until he

Keep household and garden poisons away from your Collie. Be certain they are out of reach when your Collie stands up on its hind legs.

To administer liquid medication, form a pocket by pulling out on the lower lip.

was sure we had gone, only to come back and find the pill on the floor when we were sure he had swallowed it!

Note: Avoid breaking up pills, because some pills have a protective coating important for delayed release in the intestine.

Extra care of your senior Collie will ensure the comfort it deserves.

Breeding Implications

You may have thought about breeding your Collie. If so, the concept that a dog must be bred to be psychologically fulfilled is not correct. A neutered or spayed Collie can be an outstanding companion. If you have purchased a female Collie with the thought of breeding her to recoup some of the purchase price, you are on the wrong track.

Be aware of the time and expense of raising a litter of healthy and active puppies. Both males and females will need an examination before breeding and should be up to date with all inoculations. Fecal exams will be necessary to be sure both are free from internal parasites. Females will need a prenatal exam and additional food and supplements.

Puppies will need to have a physical exam, be checked for worms, and receive inoculations. Their eyes must be examined by a qualified ophthalmologist and AKC registration papers obtained before sale. Increased amounts of food will be needed to meet the demands of both the dam and puppies. Males must be examined for sterility and any health defects.

One should carefully consider the existing overpopulation problem of all breeds of dogs and the consequences they face. Too many "cute puppies" are found in shelters today and are euthanized for lack of good homes. A healthy, happy Collie companion should be your first consideration.

Managing Your Aging Collie

As your Collie enters into its senior years, it will become less active, preferring to spend more time sleeping. It may have difficulty getting up and down the steps or from its sleeping quarters. Its legs will seem stiff as arthritis begins to affect the joints. Its appetite may or may not decrease but it will need a balanced diet of fewer calories and fat, a diet sufficient in protein, bulk, and essential minerals and vitamins. Consult with your veterinarian about the various foods manufactured for the senior dog.

There are several things you can do to make life easier for your senior citizen.

✔ Keep its bed away from drafts. Extra bedding will soften the impact of its joints against hard surfaces. A foam rubber pad, covered with a washable material, will give the dog relief and comfort.

✔ A piece of carpet for the dog to stand on while eating or drinking will keep the rear legs from slipping.

✔ Keep the teeth clean to help prevent a painful gum infection. Good oral health will help internal organs as well.

✔ Your senior dog needs to be let out more often to urinate.

✔ Keep the dog clean and well groomed. Frequently, the skin of older animals becomes dry and even scaly due to reduced activity of the oil-producing glands. If your Collie is showing evidence of skin problems, consult your veterinarian.

✔ The annual checkup and booster vaccinations are still an important part of the elderly dog's well-being.

✔ Your older Collie should have moderate exercise. Good judgment in evaluating the dog's physical condition and tolerance for daily walks is necessary. Also remember that extremes in weather are difficult for an aging dog to cope with.

Saying good-bye to an old and loyal friend is never easy.

When the End Comes

It is very hard to say good-bye to an old friend, one we have loved and that has loved us in return. Any pet that has become a member of the family will be missed. When your Collie can no longer function in a way consistent with a quality life, or when it is in pain, you owe your Collie the dignity in death you afforded it in its life. Your veterinarian can help you with your decision when the time comes. Today, euthanasia is a quick and painless procedure for your aging dog. Many veterinarians will let you stay with your dog until the end, even holding it in your arms if you wish. Don't be afraid to grieve for the loss of your Collie. It is a tribute to its life and the fact that it made its presence felt in yours. Tell any friends who can't understand your grief for "just a dog," "He wasn't just a dog—he was my Collie."

THE VERSATILE COLLIE

The Collie is a versatile breed equally suited for its many roles in service to humans. Famed as therapy and guide dogs, trackers, search-and-rescue dogs, and in drug detection, Collies have served with distinction in wars. Their valor is legendary.

Sight Dogs

Guide dogs provide independence and mobility to visually impaired people, and the Collie is particularly adapted for this because of its nurturing and protective nature. In the 1940s, a Collie breeder founded Buddies, Inc. to provide obedience-trained dogs for blind children. "Prince," the first Collie guide dog, was graduated in 1949 from Leader Dogs for the Blind in Rochester, New York. The tri-color Collie was the eyes for an award-winning lecturer and TV personality, and died saving her life.

In mid-1950, "Companion Collies for the Blind" was developed by Dr. Lee Ford, utilizing both American varieties of Collies bred to smooth-coated Collies from England. The first litter produced the first Smooth Collies in the United States, nine in total, to graduate as guide dogs. The ninth became a Collie companion to a seven-year-old child, giving him unheard-of freedom. He exhibited his precious "Thunder" to a show ring championship, a

Alert and intelligent Collies are eager to serve in many different ways.

tremendous accomplishment even for a sighted child his age.

Over the years, the less common smooth-coated variety was not readily available. Most schools lost interest in them although some schools worked with occasional donated Collie puppies with good success. One such Collie from Florida donated to the Southeastern Guide Dogs was paired with a college student with outstanding results. The student returned to her studies at the University of Florida. Becoming active in the community, both performed in a local stage production of *Annie*.

The success of the Collie was partly attributed to the need for dogs that could work with the multi-impaired and the elderly, and the total dedication and joy with which they approached their work. Southeastern Guide Dogs set up its own breeding program for Collies in 1999 and now uses them as one of their primary breeds. In 2004, Southeastern Guide Dogs' ability to effectively use the smooth-coated Collie for special needs students was recognized when it joined ranks with the prestigious International Guide Dog Federation.

A Perfect Match

The Collie's power of perception in combination with its great loyalty make it an ideal breed for assistance and therapy work.

Assistance Collies

Collies are active in many assistance areas. A Smooth Collie, graduated in Israel as an Alzheimer assistance dog, is trained to stay with early-stage Alzheimer patients. The Collie will bring them home if they become confused, or stay with them until they can be found, allowing them to remain a part of the community. Collies are used as seizure-alert and asthma-alert dogs for severely affected people and as assistance dogs for multi-impaired people. These Collies devote their every ounce of energy and concern to taking care of their human companion.

The love, patience, and continuous companionship Collies give to their masters often become critical therapeutic factors.

Pet-Facilitated Therapy

Pet-Facilitated Therapy or PFT uses animals to help people with special needs. The Collie's gentle, caring nature is particularly well suited to its role as a helpmate. Instances and reports of Collies assisting people in therapy-related capacities are commonplace. The love, patience, and continuous companionship Collies give to their masters often become critical therapeutic factors.

Dog-related therapy assistance extends to the needs of the elderly, alcoholics, and abused, autistic, and latchkey children, the terminally and mentally ill, physically disabled, and others with emotional and physical problems.

The Collie's easy transition from performing before and working with schoolchildren to joyously greeting nursing home residents is readily apparent. Nothing surpasses the companionship a Collie gives to a lonely person, sparking an interest-in-life response and a recognition that someone—a dog—cares in a nonjudgmental way.

Benefits

There are many benefits of such pet-facilitated therapy. The unique bonding and sharing reduce stressful moments, and fill the void of separations. Therapy dogs can be regular visitors or live-in residents of a home or institution. The "Lassie" image favors Collies in therapy work. Children and elderly people, sometimes fearful of being hurt by a large dog, are more receptive to interacting with Collies.

Requirements

✔ PFT dogs must offer a stable, sound temperament, and friendly disposition.
✔ They must be sociable, confident, and well-mannered, as well as trainable and adaptable

to new people, situations, surroundings, and often vexing incidents.

✔ A calm, mannerly, and obedient Collie dispels apprehension and proudly exhibits its title as a treasured Therapy Dog.

Obedience training is not mandatory for the dog to become a therapy dog. Many fanciers recommend it, however, because of the assured, confident, and concentrated conduct that results when a dog knows what is expected of it; many facilities recommend this training.

Pet-facilitated therapy is a contemporary way of establishing the human-dog relationship, interaction, and experience. There is no more rewarding experience for an owner and his or her Collie than enriching the lives of others.

Therapy-Comfort Collies

Collies were prominent among other dog breeds in the aftermath of the 9/11 terrorist attacks on the World Trade Center. An eighth-generation Lassie son named Rusty, from Oxford, New Jersey, brought comfort with a warm muzzle and cheer to the many rescue workers at the scene and to the families searching for their loved ones.

The trained therapy dog was first stationed at Pier 94 and then at Liberty State Park. Rusty sat with children who lost parents, parents who lost children, and husbands and wives who lost mates. They hugged him and wept into his ruff fur. Rusty always responded with a calming sense of reassurance and compassion. Rusty instinctively understood their grief. He was a soulmate, a friend when most needed.

For exemplary service to humankind, Rusty was named to the New Jersey Veterinary Foundation Animal Hall of Fame and recognized as

The Collie's versatility is well known.

The "Lassie" image favors Collies in therapy work.

a 9/11 Ground Zero Comfort Dog. A recipient of the American Kennel Club Canine Good Citizen Award, Rusty was also commended for "dedication and outstanding therapy work at the New Jersey Family Assistance Center" following the 9/11 terrorist attacks. For his exemplary work, the trained therapy Collie became an official American Red Cross Comfort Dog and Mascot.

The Courageous Collie

Collies are conspicuous among the most courageous dogs in America honored as the Dog Hero of the Year. Beginning in 1954, the dog performing the most outstanding act of courage leading to the saving of life or property has been nationally honored by a panel of respected judges. A male Collie, cited for bravery as the inaugural Dog Hero, was honored for saving the lives of children by leaping in front of automobiles to push the youngsters out of their paths.

The visually impaired use well-trained Collies for greater independence.

Canine courage has been equaled or exceeded through the years by countless dogs nationwide. These dogs have saved scores of lives by acts of courage that prevented drowning and alerted owners to fires and burglaries.

The number of heroes includes a Collie that saved a two-year-old girl from an enraged mother sow, another that saved a ten-year-old girl whose skirt had flamed up in a backyard trash fire, and one that herded his master's goats out of a burning barn. A Collie named Hero lived up to his name when he saved his young master from being trampled by a horse, and a Collie alerted a grandmother with limited vision to a house fire, thereby ensuring her escape to safety.

Collies care. The records of these valiant Collies are representative of the breed's exceptional and often psychic feats.

War Dogs

The training of dogs for military and police work began in continental Europe toward the end of the nineteenth century. Military author-

Coaching Collies

Though hardly renowned as a carriage dog, Collies at one time traveled with coaches, guarding the vehicle and otherwise protecting its human companions. It was observed at the turn of the century by one writer that "the Collie is admirably adapted as a companion . . . and as such he accompanies the carriage when its owner goes out for a drive; for his fondness for horses is scarcely excelled by that of the spotted coach dog." Today, although rare, Collies are occasionally glimpsed accompanying horse-drawn carriages on pleasure drives through the countryside and especially at horse shows. Reliability is important and essential with carriage dogs. The Collie's dependability is particularly suited to his work as a coach dog.

A Smooth Collie working as liaison dog.

with the American Armed Forces. Dogs also served during the Korean War, and it is believed that some 10,000 U.S. servicemen were saved by dogs during the Vietnam War.

ities trained dogs for their armed services and provided dogs for their allies. Before being sent to the battlefields after the outbreak of continental war, the dogs were given additional training for their duties as messenger, sentinels, and ambulance workers, and were exposed to smoke and gunfire.

Among other breeds, Collies were considered desirable for messenger, guardian, and sentry work because of their essential qualities of keen sense, high intelligence, courage, endurance, and trainability.

Dogs have continued to serve in every war through Desert Storm in the Persian Gulf and the Middle East. Upward of 40,000 dogs, including 20,000 in World War II have served

Collies are prominently used in therapy-related assistance capacities.

Official American Red Cross Comfort Dog and Mascot.

Search-and-Rescue Collies

Qualified dogs are registered for search-and-rescue after extensive training for lost or injured people. Training for this work is rigorous and demands intelligent and physically well-conditioned dogs. Beyond obedience discipline, the dogs' training includes guarding, swimming, and jumping over obstacles.

ACE Honors

The extraordinary canine-human bond and the innumerable ways in which dogs meaningfully contribute to our lives are honored by the American Kennel Club Awards for Canine Excellence (ACE). The impact dogs have on people's lives in their unconditional love and contribution to the well-being of humans is recognized by the annual ACE honors.

In 2004, Saber, a ten-year-old Rough Collie from Dallas, Texas, was an ACE honoree. Cross-trained in water search, scent discrimination, cadaver search, and trailing, Saber was certified as an air scent dog in urban, disaster, and wilderness work. The male Collie was a member of Mark 9 Search-and-Rescue and an original member of Texas Task Force, a statewide disaster response team. He also served with the international First Special Response Group and worked many high-profile searches such as the Force 5 tornadoes in Oklahoma and the recovery operation following the *Columbia* Space Shuttle tragedy.

Outside the spotlight, Saber became acclimated to aircraft, helicopters, and the canine harness used to lower him into otherwise inaccessible areas. This Collie participated in public awareness education programs. Reaching some 2,500 children yearly, Saber demonstrated the role of search-and-rescue dogs and helped the children understand what they should do if they become lost.

The local police department crime prevention unit cited Saber for his exceptional work with children. The ACE-winning Collie was previously named to the Oklahoma Veterinary Animal Hall of Fame for his remarkable service to humankind.

Documented Collie life-saving acts have prevented many tragedies.

After extensive training, qualified Collies are registered for search-and-rescue work.

The Drug War

Dangerous tasks such as sniffing out drugs and explosives are performed by dogs. The Honolulu Police Department had great esteem for a trained Collie, Candy, that did some astonishing work for the customs inspectors. Her owner, a department member, was observed by an official practicing scent discrimination exercises with her. They experimented and learned that the Collie could pick out marijuana from other odorous packets containing spices, tea, and coffee. At the customs office, surrounded by hundreds of packages, the female Collie pinpointed caches, helping the customs agents to track down suppliers. Candy never made a mistake.

COMPETITIVE EVENTS

In most sections of the country, there is some type of performance or conformation competition nearly every weekend. Events such as obedience trials and tracking tests are measures of the Collie's performance, while dog shows are evaluations of the dog's conformation.

Obedience Trials

Obedience Trials test a dog's ability to perform a prescribed set of exercises on which it is scored. There are three levels of Obedience classes, each more difficult than the preceding one.

Novice: The first level is "Novice." To be acceptable companions, all dogs should be trained to do a set of particular Novice exercises. Among the exercises are heeling on lead, staying on command, and coming when called. The Novice level is called Companion Dog or CD, which is the first "leg" toward an Obedience degree title and is indicated after the dog's registered name.

Open work: The next Obedience performance level is open work, with such exercises as retrieving a dumbbell, jumping a hurdle, and the broad jump. The scoring is the same as for

Agility, Herding, and Obedience Trials measure the Collie's intelligence.

Novice, and the degree earned is the Companion Dog Excellent or CDX title.

Utility work: Utility work is the most advanced level. Among the required exercises are scent discrimination and responding to hand signals, leading to the title of Utility Dog or UD. With the Utility title, a dog can continue to compete and, if successful, can become an Obedience Trial Champion or OTCh.

Tracking: Dogs passing Tracking Tests, in which a dog must follow a trail by scent, earn a TD or Tracking Dog title. Dogs passing a more advanced test can be awarded the TDX or Tracking Dog Excellent title.

Obedience training and trials are both worthwhile experiences. A dog with good manners is a good canine citizen and a welcomed member of society. The trial competition is a test of your ability as a trainer and the intelligence of your Collie. Unlike conformation competition, your dog is not judged against other dogs.

A healthy, athletic Collie performs well in all phases of Obedience work.

Agility Trials

Definitely a team sport, an Agility Trial is an event at which qualifying scores toward titles are awarded. Recognized by the American Kennel Club, Agility Trials are very popular with competitors and the public alike. The goal is to complete an obstacle course within a stated period of time with the dog's handler alongside giving directions. Obstacles are varied and may include tunnels, jumps, elevated dog walks, and more.

As a physically demanding event, for both dog and handler, Collies should receive a veterinarian "good health" clearance before undertaking this sport. Dogs must be at least ten months old to enter an Agility Trial.

Herding Trials

The first step is to determine whether your Collie has the instinct to herd. An instinct test will provide this information. Many clubs, not just for Collies, offer these tests as a way to get started.

All dogs must be nine months of age and registered with the American Kennel Club as a herding dog to enter a licensed Herding Trial. Three levels of exercises are offered at competitive Trial level:

1. Herding Started
2. Herding Intermediate
3. Herding Excellent.

There are a series of tests most handlers take with their Collies to evaluate their competence in herding prior to participating at the Trial level. Qualifying scores and Herding titles are awarded in Herding tests. At Herding Trials qualifying scores and championship points toward titles are awarded to those dogs passing a series of exercises in the level in which they are entered.

Your Collies should be in good physical condition to herd. A thorough checkup for joint problems or heart or breathing abnormalities is recommended. Herding classes and trainers may be found by contacting the American Working Collie Association, the Collie Club of America, or the American Kennel Club. Attend a Herding Test or Trial in your area. You will be fascinated to watch Collies work as they were originally bred to do.

Rally

Rally is a new AKC event that emphasizes fun in a sport for dogs, owners, and spectators. Described as highly contagious by enthusiasts, a dog and handler Rally is an event, similar to rally auto racing in which the team navigates a series of sequentially signed exercises. A photograph on each sign indicates a particular exercise. Rally judges select from 50 signs to design courses unique to each trial.

The number of required exercises is increased with each of three levels of competition—Novice, Advanced, and Excellent. All Rally Novice title exercises are performed on lead. The more challenging exercise levels—for Rally Advanced and Rally Excellence titling degrees—require off lead performance. The Rally course is worked one dog and handler team at a time. On average, the

Obedience training is a satisfying and worthwhile experience for you and your Collie.

Agility Trials are physically demanding for dog and handler.

Testing is available to determine your Collie's instinct to herd.

dog and handler are in the ring between two and two and a half minutes. Using a 100-point score, the tiebreaker is the time of the run. Good, solid performance is the objective. Unlike traditional obedience exercises, handlers may use verbal encouragement, hand signals, and body language to encourage their dog through the Rally course.

Fun Winter Sports

Skijouring and dogsledding are sheer fun and surefire winter activities for both owners and Collies. In skijouring, the Collie pulls the skier, who is on cross-country skis. The key to an easy pull is gradually introducing body weight to the dog's harness, before the skier actually assumes an upright position on skis. Apart from appropriate clothes, the equipment consists of skis, poles, dog harness, and ganglien belt or hand-held tow rope. The sport can be adapted for non-snow conditions with skies on rollers used for downhill practice, during summer months.

Collie sledding enthusiasts say their dogs love the sport. They praise sledding with their dogs and relay their impression that their dogs enjoy working with and pleasing their partners. Team size can range from one dog to several. Most starters use from one to three dogs. The major

You will be fascinated watching Collies at work.

Collies adapt well to pulling lightweight carts or sleds.

equipment used is the dog harness and sled. A three-wheeled vehicle or rig is used for no-snow conditions. A team of well-conditioned adult dogs can easily pull an average-size person. Collie sledding fanciers say it becomes increasingly difficult to hold back the dogs once they are exposed to sledding. The dogs want to go and thoroughly anticipate the experience.

Skijouring and sledding are fun and efficient ways of muscling up young Collies and toning up maturing Collies. At the same time, the fresh air and outdoor exercise serve to stimulate and invigorate both handler and dog.

The Carting Collie

The use of dogs in harness, pulling a small child or two or a light load of firewood, reappeared on the American scene during the 1970s. Carting enthusiasts, while small in number, conduct the sport in humane and orderly fashion. Collie carters report that the breed adapts quickly and responds eagerly to the opportunity.

Minimal equipment is necessary for carting. Apart from a well-maintained dog, a properly fitted cart and harness are essential. Ideally, the cart should be perfectly balanced with zero tongue weight, and should be flexible and inexpensive, a vehicle that all large and medium-size dogs can pull.

This is an event for adult dogs only. Starting a puppy in harness before full maturity could have serious consequences in its development. Talking to someone involved in carting before you begin training will help you get started correctly and avoid accidents and injuries.

UNDERSTANDING DOG SHOWS

The majority of Collies are, without a doubt, sold and owned as family pets; however, many are outstanding examples of the breed and are exhibited in competitions held around the country.

Selective breeding for the Collie as a specific breed began many years ago. When the breed was sufficiently recognized for its particular characteristics, a breed standard was written. This is the accepted "blueprint" for what a Collie should be, not only in physical terms, but in temperament as well. The standard was written keeping in mind the Collie's work as a herding dog and the necessity of soundness in movement, which is its ability to move correctly without tiring. The head and expression of the Collie are of particular importance in demonstrating type, the characteristic that makes it different or sets it apart from any other breed.

The Collie standard was written and adopted by the Collie Club of America and approved by

The tri-color Rough Collie's white mane frames its luxuriant black coat.

the American Kennel Club on May 10, 1977. You can obtain a copy of the *Official Standard for the Collie* from the American Kennel Club.

Dog Shows

In dog shows or conformation competitions each dog is judged according to a set standard or an ideal physical appearance approved for its breed. Judges compare the dogs and evaluate them according to the mental image of the correct dog.

There are two types of show in which a Collie can earn points toward the title of Champion. These are an All-Breed show, where different breeds of dogs are exhibited, and a Specialty show, for only one specific breed.

The primary purpose of a dog show is to enable owners to exhibit their dogs in competi-

Each Collie is judged according to an ideal physical appearance approved for its breed.

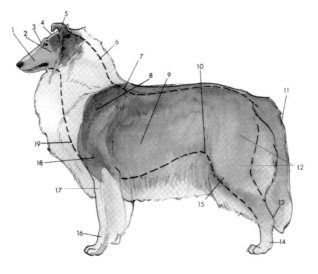

Anatomy of the Collie.

1. Muzzle
2. Cheek
3. Stop
4. Skull
5. Ear
6. Neckline
7. Withers
8. Shoulder
9. Rib cage
10. Loin
11. Tail
12. Hindquarters
13. Hock
14. Rear pastern
15. Stifle
16. Front pastern
17. Forequarters
18. Brisket
19. Chest

Collies compete with others of their kind.

A fun match gives inexperienced pups further training for a show career.

tion with others of their kind, and by using only dogs that have proved, through such competition, to be the best representatives of their breed to improve the quality of purebred dogs.

Dog shows licensed by the American Kennel Club (AKC) are subject to strict rules that must be adhered to by everyone connected with the show. All dogs must be purebred, at least six months of age, and AKC registered to enter. AKC registration means a dog, its parents, and its ancestors are purebred. Dogs are considered to be adults on the day they become one year old.

All-Breed Shows

At an All-Breed show each variety of Collies (Rough and Smooth) is judged separately in Collie classes. The winners of each variety then

Dog show judging is subjective. Remember this and be ready to try again.

Rough and Smooth Collie varieties are judged separately.

proceed to the group judging. There are seven groups into which dogs are placed, according to the work they do and the type of dog they are:

✔ Sporting
✔ Hound
✔ Working
✔ Terrier
✔ Toy
✔ Non-Sporting
✔ Herding.

Note: Both Collie varieties compete in the Herding group. The winner of each group will then compete for the coveted title of Best in Show.

Specialty Shows

Single-Breed or Specialty shows are judged in much the same way, except there is no group judging. At a Collie Specialty show, as in an All-Breed show, the Rough and Smooth varieties are judged separately. The Best of Variety Rough and the Best of Variety Smooth compete against one another for the Best of Breed. Another exception is that the puppy classes and open classes are divided by color as well as by age. Otherwise, the judging procedure is done in the same manner.

How Dogs Are Judged

✔ The judge, licensed by the AKC, must study each dog carefully according to the standard, using the hands as well as the eyes, with the dog in motion and standing still.

✔ He or she checks the texture of the coat, firmness of muscle, and overall body structure.

✔ The teeth are checked for correct alignment.

✔ The head and expression of each dog must be evaluated, including shape and position of the eye as well as ear set.

✔ The judge, guided by the breed standard, looks for the dog that in his or her opinion most nearly fills the criteria set by this standard.

✔ Placements are awarded from one through four to those dogs that best meet these requirements.

✔ The judge also must watch for definite faults that are to be discouraged or penalized.

Matches

All-Breed and Specialty clubs give matches as well as regular AKC-licensed shows. A match does not offer points toward a championship but rather acts as further training for young, inexperienced pups as well as older dogs, handlers, judges, and club officials. The dogs are divided by breed, then into classes by age and sex. A fun match will allow puppies as young as two months of age to participate, but the puppy should be inoculated before taking part in these events. This informal show is a fine opportunity

Young people learn about dog shows and junior showmanship.

for you and your Collie to learn about dog shows, and to meet people in your chosen breed.

Junior Showmanship

In some shows, there may be classes offered for Junior Showmanship. This is open to youngsters between the ages of 10 and 18. In this category the handler, rather than the dog, is judged, so no championship points are awarded. However, a first-place win entitles the boy or girl to move on to more advanced classes. Junior Showmanship is a recognized AKC event enabling young people to learn more about handling a dog, good sportsmanship, and dog shows in general.

To obtain the names of local clubs that put on dog shows, obedience trials, or other performance events contact the American Kennel Club in Raleigh, North Carolina, or visit their web site at *www.AmericanKennelClub.com.*

RESPONSIBLE DOG OWNERSHIP

As a dog owner, you know the companionship, loyalty, love, and fun that your dog adds to your life. You also must realize that owning a dog carries with it certain responsibilities.

Barking

Dog owners are sometimes insensitive to the barking of their own dog. Put yourself in your neighbors' place to see how your dog's habits affect them. Excessive barking can be extremely annoying!

In a great many areas there are laws written to prohibit a noisy animal within a particular jurisdiction. For example, a typical ordinance might read: "It shall be unlawful for any person to allow prolonged or intense barking or other harsh or excessive noises to be made by any animal under his ownership or control, at any time, so as to disturb the quiet, comfort, or repose of one or more members of the community." It is your responsibility to be familiar with all the laws in your community pertaining to dog ownership.

The breed's fabled shawl collar frames the distinctive Rough Collie's sable and white coat.

Barking, of course, can be helpful by alerting owners of potential dangers or warning of a stranger's presence. A barking dog alerts neighbors to intruders when you are not at home, or the dog's barking may indicate an animal in distress.

There are also bad aspects of a barking dog: How will you know if danger is imminent or intruders are present if your dog is allowed to bark over prolonged periods of time for no reason? One dog barking usually starts another dog barking. The noise is aggravating to neighbors, period. They have every right to demand a noise-free environment and you must do everything in your power to drastically reduce the noise. Barking always creates neighborhood arguments and resentments and sometimes leads to warrant citations. It can also be harmful to the dog. This behavior may indicate a bored or highly nervous animal. Unless stopped, barking may develop into a type of hysteria.

You can determine for yourself whether your dog is a good companion and watchdog or a neighborhood noise nuisance.

Does your dog bark excessively:

✔ when someone rings your doorbell?
✔when garbage collectors, mail carriers, or paper carriers go past your house?
✔when children are playing outside?
✔when another animal comes into view?
✔when another dog barks?
✔when hearing a siren?
✔when it wants to get into the house?
✔when you leave or return home?
✔when left alone?

If your answer is "yes" to any of these questions, your dog probably already is a neighborhood nuisance. This disturbance of the peace is one of the quickest and most common ways to become a bad neighbor. Remember: Persistent barkers are more likely to be ignored if there is a real emergency because they bark all the time.

Unnecessary barking is a nuisance and must be stopped.

Fortunately, there are steps you can take:
✔Determine what causes the dog to bark.
✔Be alert to stop the barking as soon as it starts.
✔Train your dog to respond to a command to be quiet. Try saying "Enough!" with emphasis.
✔Reward your dog whenever it barks for watchdog reasons.
✔Don't leave an animal unattended for long periods of time.
✔Train your dog to stay quietly within its quarters when you are away.

If you are concerned about a neighbor's barking dog, first try to contact the owner and work out a solution. If this does not work, you have the right to contact your local police department. If you are the owner of such a dog, talk to your neighbors and ask for their patience while you are training your dog. A spirit of cooperation can be created without hard feelings. Tell them you want to know when your dog is disturbing them and assure them you will take care of it. Dogs should be good neighbors, too.

Preventing or breaking a bad habit really depends on you. Remember to reassure your dog by petting it and talking to it when it is quiet and well behaved. It will soon learn that its silence pleases you.

The Leash

In almost all areas of the country, strict leash laws are in effect. Usually these laws require that all dogs be on a leash when not on the owner's property. This includes country and urban areas as well. It is a good rule to follow. Unfortunately, too many dog-related accidents have occurred, affecting other dogs, other animals, and people of all ages, creating the undeniable need to keep all dogs under

*Introduce leash training slowly
with a lot of praise.*

the control of a leash. Obeying leash laws will enable you to convey your sincerity in being a responsible dog owner. A leash also offers other advantages:

✔The leash is the best birth control device, preventing random matings and unwanted puppies.

✔It is the best way to keep your dog from injury, keeping your pet from darting into traffic, from dog fights, and encounters with sick or injured wild animals, eliminating pain to the dog and veterinary bills for you.

✔It is the best good-neighbor policy maker, keeping your pet from any sort of trespassing, destructive or otherwise, on your neighbor's lawn or other private land. It will also keep your pet from jumping up on children or adults and possibly inflicting injury, fright, or discomfort on them.

✔It is the best wildlife and environment protection, keeping your pet from harassing deer and other wild animals, either by himself or as part of a stray dog pack.

✔It is the best way to develop an affectionate pet, as the touch of it gives your dog definite assurance that it is protected and loved. Most dogs learn quickly that the leash is a sure sign of an outing with their friend.

✔The leash is an extension to the collar. The collar is the best identification service, as the license and rabies tags attached to the collar will get your dog back to you if it should become lost. Use them both as a matter of practice. Check with your local humane society

*Puppies left alone for too long will be
bored and will get into mischief.*

A sociable and well-mannered Collie adapts easily to new situations.

or police department about leash laws in your area.

Cleaning Up

Taking complete responsibility for your Collie includes cleaning up after your dog at home as well as in public places. Your Collie can be taught to "potty" in your own yard and not to use your neighbor's property for this purpose.

Repetition and praise on a daily schedule will help to teach and reinforce this lesson.

When you walk your dog in public places, carry plastic bags and spoons to aid in the clean-up. If proper receptacles are not available, place the bags in a paper sack and carry it home. Allowing your Collie to become a public nuisance as well as creating a health hazard is definitely not being a responsible dog owner.

Dog Parks

As our urban populations continue to grow, fewer cities and towns have green space—fields or open areas—in which to exercise our dogs. As a result many local jurisdictions have set aside dog parks. These parks are most often brought about through the efforts of dog owners who are aware of the need for dogs to not only exercise in a safe and friendly environment but to socialize and interact with other dogs and new people as well.

City and county officials cooperate with dog owners by allowing several acres of land for this purpose. Sometimes a local business will sponsor or dedicate land for a park. Fundraisers are used to offset the cost of the land and necessary maintenance. The parks have perimeter fencing with areas for free play. The areas are divided into separate spaces for different sizes and ages of dogs. Strict management is administered.

Parks will require that dogs be neutered and have up-to-date inoculation records. Dogs must be on leash to enter the park and, of course, owners must pick up after their dogs. Call your local humane society or parks department to find out if there's such a park in your area. If not, perhaps this is your opportu-

Curiosity and playfulness go hand-in-hand in a Collie puppy's life.

Dog parks and camps provide a safe place for fun and exercise.

nity to become involved in such a worthwhile undertaking. Truly, it can be a benefit for both you and your Collie while providing an enjoyable, healthy, and social activity for the whole community.

Camps for Dogs

Did you know that you and your Collie can go away to camp? Well, you can. More and more camps for dogs and their owners are sprouting up. And going to camp with your dog is becoming a popular pastime. The camps are set up in a variety of ways. Some of them are available for a short stay of a day or two, some are for weekend getaways, and others offer an extended period of time to enjoy predetermined events. These may include such activities as obedience, tracking, and herding classes. Swimming, agility, and flyball are other sports sometimes offered as well. A camp vacation allows lots of free time with your Collie and a chance to make new friends while providing a truly unique experience for all who want some time for fun and challenge.

Collies are among the thousands of dogs that have earned the title "Good Citizen."

The camps are usually owned and operated by dog lovers themselves. Some camps have counselors who offer help and guidance with the classes. For information on dog parks and dog camps check the Internet.

Canine Good Citizen Program

The American Kennel Club Canine Good Citizen Program and Test, established in September 1989, has a distinct objective. Its purpose is to demonstrate that the dog, as a companion of man, can be a respected member of the community. The goal is to educate dog owners to the benefit of a well-behaved pet. The program is specifically designed as a response to anti-canine sentiment. The AKC estimates that approximately 500,000 dogs have passed the Canine Good Citizen test since its inception.

Mixed breeds are eligible to participate at non-AKC events, since the general public does not discriminate between the purebred and non-purebred dog. Local dog obedience and training clubs administer the events while the AKC provides direction, evaluator forms, and certificates of recognition. Before completing the test requirements, the dog's owner must present a current rabies certificate and any other state or locally required inoculation certificates and license.

To successfully qualify, the dog must complete ten steps that demonstrate confidence and control:

Appearance and grooming. Demonstrates that the dog welcomes being groomed and examined and will permit a stranger such as a veterinarian, assistant, or someone other than the owner to do so.

Accepting a stranger. The evaluator and handler shake hands and exchange pleasantries. The dog must show no sign of resentment or shyness, and must not break position or try to go to the evaluator.

Walking on loose lead or out for a walk. Demonstrates that the handler is in control. The dog must be on the left side of the handler. The dog need not be in the "heel" position as required by the AKC Obedience Tests.

A Collie puppy is always ready for play.

Walk through a crowd. The dog should have no difficulty in moving about pedestrian traffic. Dog and handler will walk around and pass close to several persons (at least three). Dog may show some interest in the strangers, but should continue to walk with the handler without evidence of shyness or resentment. The dog should not be straining at the leash.

Sit for exam. Dog allows the approach of a stranger and permits petting. The dog must not show shyness or resentment.

Sit and down on command. Dog has had some formal training and will respond to the handler's command. The evaluator must determine if the dog does respond to the handler's command. The handler may not force the dog into either position. The handler may use more than one command.

Stay in position (sit or down). Dog assumes and remains in the position commanded by the handler. The dog must maintain the position in which it was left until the handler returns and until the evaluator instructs the handler to release the dog.

Relation to another dog. Demonstrates proper behavior when in the presence of other dogs. The dog should demonstrate no more than casual interest. The dog should not go to the other dog or handler.

Reactions to distractions. The dog is confident at all times when faced with distracting conditions. The dog may express natural interest and curiosity and may startle but should not panic, try to run away, show aggressiveness, or bark.

Dog left alone. The dog is left alone, demonstrating training and good manners. The dog

Collies are normally strong, healthy dogs with relatively few problems.

should not bark, whine, howl, or pace unnecessarily or register anything other than mild agitation or nervousness.

For program and testing places, dates, and specific Canine Good Citizenship information, contact the American Kennel Club.

COLLIE ORGANIZATIONS

Considering how popular the Collie is, it's not surprising that a number of different Collie organizations exist. Although each has its own agenda, they all aim to foster awareness of and promote the breed.

Collie Club of America

The Collie Club of America, one of the oldest United States parent breed clubs, defines the Collie Standard, promotes and popularizes the Rough and Smooth Collie varieties, encourages true type Collie breeding, and conducts a Collie public education program.

The history of the Collie Club of America (CCofA) is a record of the Collie's popularity in the United States. Collies were shown at the New York City Westminster Kennel Club all-breed dog show in 1878. Interest and breeding activity grew rapidly, and on August 26, 1886, the Collie Club of America was founded. One of the oldest parent clubs, it is only two years younger than the American Kennel Club, and in 1888 became the third member club to join the AKC.

CCofA seeks to define and guard the modern Collie Standard. Its constitution established

Herding instincts are still very much a part of the Collie's personality.

several important objectives: "to promote and popularize the two varieties of Collies, to promote and encourage the breeding of true-type Collies, and the dissemination of knowledge regarding the same." Fostering ethical conduct and sportsmanship among its members and the Collie fancy at large is among its goals.

Organization: CCofA consistently has one of the nation's largest parent club memberships and is governed by a complement of officers and directors elected by the members. These include a president, two vice-presidents, secretary, treasurer, three directors-at-large, American Kennel Club delegate, and district directors from each state or area meeting minimum membership requirements. The incumbents in these positions comprise the club's executive committee, which decides policy and votes on all important business before the club. Each district director acts as a liaison between its members and the club.

Membership: Any person favorable to the objectives of the club and in good standing

Collies have a natural sweet and gentle nature.

with the American Kennel Club is eligible to apply for membership. The application must be signed by two members who know the applicant and the director from his or her state

Smooth blue merle Collie.

district. By signing, the applicant acknowledges acceptance of the club's code of ethics.

Activities: A CCofA national specialty show is held each spring in a different part of the country and annually draws entries ranging from 500 to 700 Collies. A record entry of more than 1,000 Collies was set in Chicago at the club's Centennial show. A local Collie club is usually host to the show, which rotates among six continental zones.

An obedience trial, herding instinct testing, and a herding trial are held in conjunction with the national specialty show. There also are educational seminars on various subjects of interest to breeders and judges.

CCofA presents trophies at its national show and to local Collie clubs for presentation at their specialty shows.

Numerous voluntary committees carry out the work of the club, from research to publications, from show rules to ethical conduct, to other individual projects.

Publications and Services: With a decade's old tradition of membership service, CCofA sponsors an excellent continuing education program. The club prepares and distributes, at a nominal charge, material on all phases of Collie breeding, care, training, and showing. All members receive six bi-monthly magazines and an annual report. The CCofA *Bulletin* contains informative articles, reports from the officers, and pictures of winning Collies in breed and other competition.

One of the best breed and member information sources is the *CCofA Yearbook.* Issued

*The tri-color puppy is an adorable youngster
with promise of great fun for the family.*

annually, it contains feature articles of lasting
value, officers' and committee reports, statisti-
cal data on new title holders, show results, and
photos of the year's winning Collies. Its particularly valuable reference is the geographical
and alphabetical directory of the club's several
thousand members from virtually all the states
and many countries.

The club publishes numerous pamphlets and
booklets on subjects such as puppy care and
selection, whelping, ring training for showing
Collies, junior showmanship, basic grooming,
ear care, and stud dog management. Other
club publications include comprehensive materials on obedience training, herding instinct
testing, and herding trials. Lavishly illustrated
hard-bound books record *American Collie
Champions* in a multi-volume, award-winning
series spanning more than a century of Collie
competition in America.

CCofA's audio-visual library maintains an
extensive lending library of educational video-
tapes, motion pictures and color slides of
national specialty shows, breeder profiles, and
other subjects which may be rented by clubs or
individuals for a nominal fee.

Collie Health Foundation

One of the pioneering national parent club
breed health foundations, the Collie Health
Foundation (CHF) was organized in 1986 as the
Collie Club of America Health Foundation. Its
purpose is to raise money to support grants for
research and other projects for the betterment
of the Collie and other breeds in general.

Contributions to the foundation are tax
deductible to the extent allowed by law.

The CHF is among the leading breed health
foundations and a model for many parent

*Correct eye placement and tipped ears give
the Collie a beautiful expression.*

The Collie is a descendant of one of the oldest types of pastoral dogs.

clubs. Its success helped establish the idea for the creation of the AKC Canine Health Foundation. CHF members and their money support works that are carried out across the country in some of the leading research centers for the benefit of the breed and dogs in general. The CHF has awarded thousands of dollars in total grant research funds each year for almost two decades.

The foundation activities support both educational and research activities: to promote appreciation and knowledge of Collies and dogs in general and to establish a national data base of resource materials about Collies. Its research grants focus on health problems,

genetics, breeding, and history. Publication and distribution of educational materials is an important activity and includes such topics as care, treatment, breeding, health, development, and training.

Individuals and clubs who have made the minimum membership contribution are the backbone of the foundation. Additional contributions are often received as a result of fundraising projects and donations. Officers are elected from among the membership to serve a three-year term. From these voting corporate members, not to exceed 45, a board of 15 directors and officers is elected, each person serving a three-year term. There are no paid

The hallmark of all Collies is "the look": the expression of a noble, sweet-tempered breed.

positions within the foundation. Overhead expenses such as postage and printing are reimbursed as incurred and authorized by the board. The foundation works because volunteers give of their time and talent to it. See the Collie Club of America web site to learn more about both organizations.

American Smooth Collie Association

The Smooth Collie variety in America and the American Smooth Collie Association owe their existence to the dedication of Margaret Haserot who sought out and imported the first of the variety from England. Together with the early, loyal followers of the variety, she promoted the Smooth Collie. It was in the mid-1920s that these fanciers imported Smooth, but Miss Haserot alone had the fortitude to weather the early years of unsuccessful breeding. Her interest in the variety continued unabated and in time, as more breeders became interested, she supplied good breeding stock.

The need for communication and organization among the Smooth enthusiasts became apparent as well as a link to comradeship. The outgrowth of this informality was the organization of the American Smooth Collie Association in 1957. The aim of the club was to promote better quality dogs and to encourage breeding, exhibiting, and the training of Smooth Collies.

With a half-century of service to the breed and its fanciers, the club continues its goal of promoting the Smooth Collie. The club pub-

lishes a quarterly magazine dedicated to the variety and voices the news and views of its several hundred members. The club holds a biannual convention where Smooth enthusiasts can gather for the business meeting but, most important, for a chance to share their love of the variety.

The Smooth Collie variety has assumed parity with the Rough Collie variety and has taken its place within breed competition as well as in the popularity of the public. Smooth fanciers like to proclaim, "Half the work and all of the fun!"

American Working Collie Association

Established in 1979, the American Working Collie Association (AWCA) is dedicated to the promotion and preservation of the Collie as a

An intent gaze is front and center of the Collie's distinctive appearance.

The young tri-color Rough Collie is at home among the bales of straw in farm country.

working breed. This goal is accomplished in a number of ways such as developing and implementing programs designed to demonstrate and test the variety of talents the breed possesses in such activities as herding, sledding, agility, and carting. AWCA encourages opportunities for the breed such as the use of Collies as service dogs for the physically impaired and as guide dogs. The association also acts as a clearinghouse of information about the working Collie.

AWCA's most well-known effort is the Collie Herding Program. The first herding program available to the breed, it offers a means of testing for basic herding instinct and a method for preserving the Collie herding trait. Begun in 1984, the AWCA program enabled clubs and individuals to sponsor herding instinct certification test and trials.

This pioneering effort was ultimately instrumental in gaining the American Kennel Club's recognition of herding as a performance event in the summer of 1989. At that time, only a few national breed clubs had established herding programs—Collies, Bearded Collies, and the Belgian Tervurens. For those breeds without a program, a new club, the American Herding Breeds Association, was founded to handle their sanctions and certifications. Subsequently, the AKC herding program was revised and expanded, taking into consideration the various breeds and their manner of working livestock. The AWCA herding program continues to function apart from the other national herding programs.

The AWCA Versatility Program, established in 1984, recognizes Collies that demonstrate versatile working ability. These achievements are awarded Versatility Companion and Versatility Companion Excellent titles. Performance includes work activities like obedience, herding,

A mature Rough Collie displays a beautiful sable and white coat.

draft (sledding, weight pulling, carting), tracking, and other activities such as pet-assisted or therapy work, the Canine Good Citizen Test, and lure coursing. The AWCA also offers a Carting Program and awards appropriate recognition with Carting and Carting Excellent titles.

AWCA members are very active in competitive and performance events. Some have done television commercials and media advertising with their Collies. Many members are involved with their dogs in community activities such as visits to nursing or convalescent homes and education demonstrations of pet care and training as well as breed rescue.

White Collie Club

Organized in 1970, the White Collie Club (WCC) has worked for more than three decades for the betterment of the breed. Using the motto "Quality First, Color Second," the White Collie Club dedicates its efforts "to promoting the lovely white coat color in Collies as an enhancement to Collie type." Membership in the WCC is open to anyone who believes quality white Collies can be, and should be, as fully appreciated as the other recognized Collie colors. Many members also have concurrent membership in the Collie Club of America and other Collie organizations and take part in conformation and performance events.

WCC has produced a bi-monthly newsletter for its membership focusing on Collies in general and whites in particular. The club also publishes periodic yearbooks, a color chart, and information about breeding white Collies.

Collie Club of Canada

In its third decade of service to the breed and its fanciers, the first national specialty show of the Collie Club of Canada (CCC) was held in 1986 in Winnipeg, Manitoba, followed by a successful show every year since.

The CCC's governing body is composed of 10 area directors that act as liaison between the membership and the executive committee. Area directors are responsible for promoting the Collie and the club within their area, by hosting matches, herding clinics, and writing columns for national publication. Area directors also form Collie rescue programs within their area that are regarded as a national program.

The Canadian Collie Standard is slightly different from its United States counterpart, with some minor discrepancies, but it essentially recognizes the Rough and Smooth varieties of Collie.

2 INFORMATION

Organizations

American Veterinary Medical Association
930 North Meacham Road
Schaumberg, IL 60173

American Working Collie Association
208 Harris Road, FA 1
Bedford Hills, NY 10507
(914) 241-7094
www.awa.net

Collie Club of America
47 Kielwasser Road
Washington Depot, Ct. 06794
(860) 868-2863
ccasec@snet.net
www.collieclubofamerica.org

The Collie Health Foundation
Lori Montero, Secretary
10508 Knox Avenue
Matthews, NC 28105
www.colliehealth.org/index.html

Collie Welfare / Rescue
E-mail: *Heathrri669@aol.com*

Canine Eye Registration Foundation
South Campus Court, Building C
West Lafayette, IN 47907

Guide Dog Foundation
(800)548-4337
www.guidedog.org

Orthopedic Foundation for Animals
2300 Nifong Boulevard
Columbia, MO 65201

Therapy Dogs International
88 Bartley Road
Flanders, NJ 07836
(973) 252-9800
www.tdi-dog.org

Kennel Clubs

The American Kennel Club (AKC)
5580 Centerview Drive
Raleigh, NC 27606
(919) 237-9767
www.AKC.org

A new and wonderful adventure awaits you and your Collie puppy.

The Collie is a dog for all seasons.

Australian National Kennel Council
Royal Show Grounds
Ascot Vale
Victoria, Australia

Canadian Kennel Club
89 Skyway Avenue, Suite 100
Etobicoke, Ontario M9W 6R4, Canada

Irish Kennel Club
41 Harcourt Street
Dublin 2, Ireland

New Zealand Kennel Club
P.O. Box 523
Wellington 1, New Zealand

The Kennel Club
1-4 Clargis Street, Picadilly
London W7Y 8AB, England

United Kennel Club (UKC)
100 East Kilgore Road
Kalamazoo, Michigan 49001-5598

About the Authors

Hal and Mary Sundstrom have bred and shown their champion Collies in Hawaii and coast to coast. They have an extensive background in many phases of the dog world. Both are recipients of national good sportsmanship, writing, and public education awards. They have edited and published purebred dog books and magazines and served as breed consultants to Salamander and Quarto Publishing of London. Mary is past director and Hal past president of the Collie Club of America, its health foundation, and the Dog Writers' Association of America and Dog Writers' Educational Trust. The Sundstroms and their homebred Rough Collies, Harrison and Zachary, live in horse country USA: Ocala, Florida.

Acknowledgments

We would like to thank Fredric L. Frye, DVM, MSC, FRSM, for his assistance on the first edition. We dedicate this book to the Collie breed and to our own Halamar Collies that have brought us so much joy over the years. To Pat Hunter, our editor at Barron's, we say, "Thank you."

Cover Photos

Front and back covers: Norvia Behling; inside front and inside back covers: Tara Darling.

Photo Credits

Akin-Fowler Studio: page 60; Norvia Behling: pages 10 (bottom), 11, 12, 13, 16, 17, 21, 22 (top), 26, 31, 34, 37 (left), 44, 45, 46, 49, 52 (top), 57 (bottom), 58, 77 (both), 79, 82, 83; Kent Dannen: pages 7, 8, 19, 20, 25, 29, 30, 36, 37 (right), 43, 48, 50, 52 (bottom), 53, 54, 59, 61 (top), 62, 66 (both), 67, 68, 69, 70, 71 (both), 72, 73, 75, 80, 84, 85, 86 (both), 87 (both), 90 (both), 91, 92, 93; Tara Darling: pages 4, 9, 10 (top), 14, 18, 22 (bottom), 23, 28, 42, 47, 57 (top), 78, 81, 88, 89; Cheryl Ertelt: pages 24 (top), 63, 64, 65 (both); Pets by Paulette: pages 5, 15, 35, 39, 51, 55, 74; Harold Sundstrom and Mary Sundstrom: pages 2–3, 24 (bottom), 38, 61 (bottom).

© Copyright 2005, 1994 by Barron's Educational Series, Inc.

All inquiries should be addressed to:
Barron's Educational Series, Inc.
250 Wireless Boulevard
Hauppauge, NY 11788
www.barronseduc.com

ISBN-13: 978-0-7641-2859-2
ISBN-10: 0-7641-2859-0

International Standard Book No. 0-7641-2859-0

Library of Congress Catalog Card No. 2004066225

Library of Congress Cataloging-in-Publication Data
Sundstrom, Harold Walter, 1929–
    Collies / Harold W. Sundstrom & Mary O.
    Sundstrom.
        p. cm. — (A Complete pet owner's manual)
    Includes bibliographical references and index.
    ISBN 0-7641-2859-0
        1. Collie. I. Sundstrom, Mary O. II. Title. III. Series.

SF429.C6S86   2005
636.737'4—dc22   2004066225

Printed in China
9 8 7 6 5 4